– FIRST EDITION

P9-CKF-535

Caught in the CROSSHAIRS
– A True Eastern Oregon Mystery –

Other Books
by Rick Steber

Rendezvous
Traces
Union Centennial
Where Rolls the Oregon
Heartwood
Oregon Trail – Last of the Pioneers
Roundup
New York to Nome
Wild Horse Rider
Buckaroo Heart
No End in Sight
Buy the Chief a Cadillac
Legacy
Forty Candles
Secrets of the Bull

Tales of the Wild West Series
Oregon Trail
Pacific Coast
Indians
Cowboys
Women of the West
Children's Stories
Loggers
Mountain Men
Miners
Grandpa's Stories
Pioneers
Campfire Stories
Tall Tales
Gunfighters
Grandma's Stories
Western Heroes

www.ricksteber.com

RICK STEBER

– A True Eastern Oregon Mystery –

Published by – TWO STAR –
An imprint of Bonanza Publishing
PO Box 204
Prineville, OR 97754

All rights reserved. No part of the material protected by this
copyright notice may be reproduced or utilized in any form or by
any means, electronic or mechanical, including photocopying,
recording or by any informational storage and retrieval system
without written permission from the copyright owner.

Cover photo by Larry Turner – www.larryturnerphotography.com
Cover design by Gary Asher
Book design by Jody Conners

ISBN: 978-0-945134-39-8

Copyright © 2011, by Rick Steber

PRINTED IN THE UNITED STATES OF AMERICA
FIRST EDITION

DEDICATION

To Keith Baker and Dave Rouse.
They never gave up in their quest for justice.

"Injustice never rules forever...."

— Seneca, Roman philosopher

CHAPTER 1

The Search

On the last day of summer a deadly dance unfolds on the sprawling landscape of timbered hills and open sagebrush country that defines Eastern Oregon. A curious cowboy on a green broke horse, cow dog trotting faithfully alongside moves slowly, cautiously, down the spine of a rocky ridge. The cowpoke slips from the saddle, takes the lead rope in one hand and squints through a narrow opening between tightly packed trees and into the swale below. Then he squats on his haunches, takes a can of snuff from his shirt pocket and tucks a fat pinch of brown tobacco under his bottom lip. He replaces the lid, adjusts his hat to shade his eyes from the setting sun, and continues to intently stare downhill; hoping to see what he might see, expecting something to happen, not at all sure what that something might be. The lead rope remains in his right hand, the snuff can in his left. Behind him the horse blows a soft trill of air out quivering nostrils and begins to anxiously paw the ground. The dog at his side, alert to danger, cocks an ear and points it down the hill.

A person takes a rest against a weathered stump, or it might have been against a tree, sights through the riflescope and lines up the crosshairs on a big bull elk that is not there, or sees the

1

target all too well. This person flips off the safety and makes a conscious decision, sending a command impulse snaking down long, pliant arm muscles to an index finger. The finger curls imperceptibly against the fine grooved metal of a trigger, curls a tiny bit more and this sets in motion a sequence of reactions that, once initiated, can never be stopped, or reversed, or taken back. Sear mechanism trips, releasing the spring-loaded hammer whose sharp point abruptly contacts the soft brass coating of the primer. Nitrogen powder ignites. Smokeless gunpowder explodes and drives the 150-grain projectile down the throat of the barrel. Lands and grooves force the bullet to twist at a ratio of one full spin to each nine inches it travels. And, as if a precise line had been drawn to the target, the bullet travels in a slight arc and slams with an abrupt thud into the cowboy's chest. Body mass absorbs the brunt force, and as the roar of the rifle washes over him, the cowboy rocks onto his heels and begins to fall, almost gently, so that when his head makes contact with the ground his hat remains in place, although the front brim is tilted upward at an odd angle. His right knee stays upright. The fingers on his left hand deftly relax and the snuff can rolls away down the incline. Overcome with panic, the horse rears, breaking off dead limbs from the tree above her head, pulls the lead rope free, and in her confusion races headlong down the rocky ridge toward where the shooter remains hidden. The dog shies, but only for a moment and then comes scooting back on his belly to whimper, whine and to finally lick the face of the dead cowboy.

Phil Brooks was a rangy man, 6 feet 2 inches and 190 pounds, a boy really, and on the day he was killed—September 20, 1994—he was only twenty-three years old. His eyes were blue, his hair was cut short and he was dressed in western garb; pretty much what he always wore because, after all, he was a cowboy. He had pointy-toed boots with slanted buckaroo riding heels, Wrangler jeans in need of a wash and held in place with a hand-tooled brown leather belt adorned with a silver rodeo buckle, no underwear, lightweight shirt with the sleeves snagged off at the elbows, and a gray felt cowboy hat that had been scuffed and banged around from wrecks on horseback, wrestling calves and rangy cows, bar fights and occasionally tossed aside when Phil was lucky enough to join a lady friend in bed.

Phil worked as a ranch hand on the Fopiano, a 33,000 acre cattle ranch on Waterman Flat in Eastern Oregon, located midway between Prineville and John Day. The Collins brothers, Jimmy and Bob, owned this ranch and several others. Jimmy and his wife Georgia lived at the Fopiano headquarters while Bob and his wife Ruth lived on the adjoining 101 Ranch.

On the day Phil was to die he spent his morning working cattle with Jimmy, and even though Jimmy was an old man, in his 80s, he was still capable of putting in long days in the saddle. He wanted to get the cattle out of the mountains and down to the safety of the barbwire delineation on Waterman Flat before hunting season began and some stupid hunter mistook a twelve hundred pound bred Hereford cow for a buck, or a bull elk.

When they broke for lunch Phil asked, "Anything pressing needs to get done?"

"Nothing that can't wait," replied Jimmy. "Got something in mind you wanna do this afternoon?"

"Was kinda thinkin'," drawled Phil, "I might take my sister's horse for a ride." He went on to explain he had picked up the horse from his sister, Tina Bolton, that it was green broke and spooky as all get-out at everything from a song bird flushing from sagebrush, to tree limbs and even shadows. The horse, a 2-year-old filly, was dark chestnut with a white blaze running from its ears down the forehead to the tip of its nose. He said the horse's name was Flirt, and followed that up with, "Sounds like somethin' a gal might come up with for a name." He shook his head. "Thought I might make a run up into the timber. Try and work out some of her spookiness." He paused for a moment to dig a final dip of chew from the can, and he reminded himself to get a fresh can when he got to his trailer. He went on. "That horse is just a little bitty thing. Hell, I'll

3

probably hafta hold up my knees or my feet'll drag the ground."
He laughed.

Jimmy said to go, take the afternoon off, that they'd ride
for more cattle in the morning. Phil got in his pickup and
drove to what was known locally as the granary, a barn where
Phil had parked his travel trailer and was living at the time.
He stopped long enough to grab a fresh can of chew and to fix
a sandwich that he took with him and ate on the way. Jimmy,
who was headed out to visit a neighbor, passed Phil on the
road and they exchanged compulsory nods. That was the last
time Jimmy saw Phil alive. Later, when Jimmy was asked what
time they had met on the road, he thought for a minute and
replied, "Suppose it was somewhere around 2 p.m., thereabouts
anyway."

⊕ ⊕ ⊕

The following day Phil's pickup was still parked at the
ranch, but Phil and the little filly, Flirt, and his cow dog,
Poncho, were nowhere to be seen. At first Jimmy didn't think
much about it, figuring his ranch hand had swung by one of
the neighbors' homes at dinnertime, as was Phil's bachelor
custom to do. After eating, if the neighbor had something to
drink, Phil probably had gotten his nose wet, as was also his
custom to do, and he was probably sleeping off a hangover. It
was as simple as that, figured Jimmy.

By midmorning, when Phil had still not returned, Jimmy
did become concerned. He went to the house and instructed
Georgia to make a few phone calls. There were half a dozen
family, friends and neighbors within a 10 mile radius and Phil
could have ridden to any of their homes and spent the night.
But no one had seen Phil and when Georgia informed her
husband of that, Jimmy shook his head side-to-side and his
voice took on a worried tone as he said, "Hope to hell that
horse didn't go down with him. Hate to think of him lying out
all night with a busted leg. Best pass the word, see if we can
get some folks to help search. Call Jim and Joyce and tell them."

4

Justin Brooks, Phil's brother, cowboyed on the nearby Scott Ranch. He recalled when Jimmy told him the news that Phil hadn't come home. His first reaction, "Shit happens out west." His second, "Figured Phil got in a horse wreck. I loaded up my horse and went to have a look. Didn't take long to cut his tracks. They was easy to follow. The horse he was riding was this dinky son-of-a-bitch, had on triple ought shoes. Nobody in this country rides a triple ought. But the ground was dry as bone and I had to work to stay on the track. My big problem was, there wasn't no logic to the way Phil was riding. He went wherever in hell he wanted to go. One time he chased some elk; must have been trying to get a look and see if there were any horns. He was out just fartin' around.

"Phil and I pretty much ride the same way. We sing, you know, something western; might be an old-time tune, might be something kinda modern. Not loud, easy like. Keeps the horse quiet. Passes time. I rode along following the tracks, singing, humming now and then, rolling over in my mind what might have happened to Phil. I kept coming to the conclusion the horse—that squirrelly little son-of-a-bitch—had gone down and Phil was lying out there with a busted leg or a concussion. It never entered my head he might be dead."

Justin followed Flirt's tracks for a couple hours, working his way around a prominent ridge near Bearway Meadow on a skid trail that was overgrown with trees, maybe fifteen or twenty years old. From there, it was pretty much a straight shot back to the ranch. On the hard-packed dry ground the tracks were difficult to follow and then they disappeared and Justin couldn't seem to find them again.

"By that time a lot of people had joined in the search, and when riders came up, I told them to stay the hell away and quit contaminatin' the area," said Justin. "I didn't need no more horse tracks to contend with."

Jimmy Collins and Pat Perry, a longtime friend of the Brooks family, arrived on foot and tried to help Justin locate tracks. But with darkness coming on fast, Jimmy said he was tired and was going back to the pickup. Pat stayed with Justin for another half hour and then he followed Jimmy back toward the pickup.

⊕ ⊕ ⊕

That afternoon word that Phil was missing had circulated quickly. A steady stream of friends and neighbors wheeled stock trucks and pickups and horse trailers into the barn lot at Fopiano headquarters, and when that was full they parked along the road. Horses were unloaded and men and women rode off into the hills to search for any sign of Phil Brooks.

Even before the searchers arrived, Jimmy Collins and Pat Perry were driving the roads, looking for tire tracks or horse tracks at all the gates. Pat recalled, "I remember when we got to what we call the bone gate—it has a leg bone off a dead cow twisted in the wire high up to keep the posts from folding back—and it was not locked. There were tire tracks there, but the ground was dry and it was impossible to tell if they were fresh or old."

While the search continued, Georgia and Jeanie Perry, Pat's wife, stayed at headquarters. Phil's parents, Jim and Joyce Brooks, arrived and Jim rode off in search for his son while Joyce went to the ranch house.

"We did our best to stay positive, wanting to believe Phil would be found, maybe injured but at least alive. There was no reason not to think that," said Jeanie. "But time was wasting. I wanted to get the police involved, have search and rescue come in and organize things and get an airplane to fly over the ranch. But there was some bad blood between the Brooks family and the local authorities, and Joyce didn't want to make that decision and risk Jim being mad about it."

The problem between Jim Brooks and Wheeler County Sheriff, Otho Caldera, stemmed from a run-in after the Spray Rodeo. That year Tina was a rodeo princess and Jim and Bob Keys were doing a little too much celebrating. Otho spotted the pickup and horse trailer weaving as Jim drove home and he threw on the overheads. As soon as Otho made contact it was obvious Jim had been drinking. In fact he had an open container tucked between his legs and he made no effort to conceal it. Otho wanted Jim to take a field sobriety test. Jim told the sheriff to go piss up a rope. That didn't set well with Otho. He announced Jim was under arrest for drunk driving, loaded him in the back of his patrol car, and according to the story that made the rounds, when they reached the café/grocery store at Service Creek, Jim said, "Whoa, we gotta stop here."

Otho asks what for. Jim responded, "Gotta buy some beer. I can't drive all the way to Fossil without a beer."

Jim kept right on talking, telling Otho his family was used to eating steaks every meal and as long as Otho had Jim locked up in jail it would be the county's responsibility to provide his family with food that was at least equal to what Jim provided them. All the way to town Jim kept up the steady banter, harassing Otho, and when they arrived at the historic brick courthouse in Fossil, Otho led Jim to the lone cell, inviting Jim to step inside and suggesting he sleep it off.

Bob Keys doubled back and bailed Jim out of jail. Even though it was the thing a friend would do, should do, it still didn't set well with Jim. He demanded to know how his buddy, who had been drinking alongside him all day, could drive to town, post bail and not get in a lick of trouble. Otho pushed Jim out the door to get rid of him, but in the aftermath, at the court hearing, Jim was fined and had his license revoked. He told Otho, "Whether or not I have a license don't mean shit. I've gotta work. I'm gonna keep driving and you better not stop me."

And Otho never did stop him. But that incident, and several more minor run-ins, led to a certain amount of animosity, hard feelings and distrust between the Brooks family and the sheriff's office. Joyce took a lot of convincing, but finally she came around and said she supposed it would be all right for Jeanie to call in a missing person's report on Phil. Within the hour, Otho and his deputy, Craig Ward, came to the ranch.

⊕ ⊕ ⊕

Sandy Edgeman's parents owned the Dollarhide Ranch east of Mitchell, and each spring the Brooks family faithfully attended the Dollarhide brandings. When Sandy was notified Phil was missing, and having grown up with an appreciation for western traditions, she dropped everything she was doing, loaded her horse in the stock trailer, and drove to Waterman Flat to lend a hand in the search.

"I've known Phil since he was just a pup," said Sandy. "He was this fun-loving kid, real outgoing, always very polite and nice when he was around me. I heard he was missing and figured I'd do what I could to help out. I'm used to being in the mountains. I get paid to ride for cattle, that's my job. When you've spent your whole life on a horse in the hills, you notice things, little things, and I figured I had a good a chance to find him.

"I drove to the Fopiano and was told there were plenty of riders searching north of the lake. The sheriff was heading up the search and he told me to start south of the bone gate and ride west. I unloaded my horse and it didn't take long to cross the open flat, reach timber and start climbing into the hills. As I went, I kept checking for tracks. There was a lot of elk sign and several times I saw elk moving out in front of me. I figured, with all the people searching, the elk were running here and there, trying to find a safe place to hunker down.

"Coming up a long draw I heard a strange noise, real low and guttural. I couldn't tell if it was an animal or whether it might be human. I pulled up, and heard it again. The only way I can describe the sound is to say it was somewhere between a grunt, a moan, and a cough. It wasn't like anything I'd heard before. At first I thought it must be a bull elk. They make some weird noises when they're in the rut. But thinking it also might be Phil groaning in pain, I went to investigate. I turned my horse uphill. We wound our way through mahogany thickets and scattered juniper and pine trees. It was brushy and steep, too.

"All of a sudden, real close, an elk cut loose with a bugle and that struck me as an odd thing—the elk I'd seen were all moving to get away, not calling—and this was an absolute perfect bugle. Ahead of me the ground leveled off onto a little bench and a clearing. I ducked down to come under a tree limb, was concentrating on the ground and searching for sign, and when I looked up, right there in front of me at the far end of this little clearing, maybe 40 yards away, was a man crouching in the shadows. He held a bow in front of him. The string was pulled back to his chin. An arrow—I saw the four blades of the broad head, saw them very distinctly—was pointed directly at me. Petrified me. My heart pounded. I cried out, "Don't shoot!"

I must have flinched, blinked, glanced away, something, I don't know. But the man was gone and all I could think was he had ducked behind a tree and dropped down into the brush. Stupid me. I rode over to where he had been and listened to see if I could hear him running away. Normally, if an animal is escaping, branches pop and rocks roll, but there was nothing, not a sound. I hollered, 'This is private property. You're not supposed to be here. You better get out. You're trespassing.'

"Still nothing, dead silence. And then it hit me how incredibly crazy I was acting. There was a man out there with a bow. He had pointed an arrow at me. I wasn't armed. I panicked, reined my horse around and left in a hurry.

"Coming off that ridge I played out the events in my mind, exactly what I had seen—the very white face, clean shaven, no glasses, dark hair—and in my mind it seemed like he was dressed casually, blue jeans and a short-sleeved shirt—definitely not painted with camo like a lot of hunters will do. But then again, it had been such a quick look, and then he was gone. I did have the impression I had scared him every bit as badly as he scared me, and that gave me a small measure of comfort.

"When I got off the hill and found a road, I located a winterkill cow, and made a triangular affair with three rib bones pointing to where I had encountered the bow hunter. I figured Jimmy and Bob Collins would want to know about the trespasser and the cow bones would direct them to the site. As

I rode on back toward the ranch I could not seem to get rid of this haunting feeling that Phil had encountered a similar situation, and that he had been dry gulched by a bow hunter. I kept pushing my horse faster and faster."

⊕ ⊕ ⊕

Tina Bolton, Phil's stepsister, purchased Flirt, a registered quarter horse, when the filly was only 5 months old. Tina recalled, "She was my baby. When she was old enough to ride I put in as much time as I could with her, mostly at play days at the Jefferson County Fairgrounds and a few times I rode on the National Grasslands east of town.

"I spoiled that horse, and I have to admit she was a tad spooky. When something got to her, like a shadow of a tree, she sucked up her butt and acted squirrelly. There was no way I had the time in my busy schedule to ride her every day like she needed to be ridden. One time Phil was visiting and I told him, 'Why don't you take her? It'd do her a world of good to be worked every day.'

"Phil was hesitant because Flirt was so small. He put me off. But the very next weekend—this would have been just a couple days before he disappeared—he returned to Madras and stayed with my sister, Wendy Chancellor. He team roped with Wendy and her husband, Larry, and at one point he told Wendy if something should happen to him he wanted two things: to be buried with what Grandpa Parton gave him, and loud music played at his funeral. He said his funeral should be happy, not sad. Wendy made light of what he was telling her, shined him on, saying, 'What are you talking about? You're 23 years old. You're not gonna die.' Phil told her he was serious and to remember what he was saying. Wendy thought this was highly uncharacteristic behavior for Phil, because he was always such a happy-go-lucky kid.

"On Sunday evening Phil swung by our place and said he was going to swap his mare, Sox, for Flirt. He promised when he brought Flirt back, she'd be as gentle as a bottle-fed lamb.

I was happy he was taking her but reminded him Flirt was a pasture horse, not used to the backcountry. I told him he'd have to have patience with her, teach her how to place her feet in the rocks, and I warned him not to ram and jam her as Phil typically did with his horses.

"Back that spring, on Memorial Day, Phil had taken Bill and I on a riding tour of the Fopiano. We were looking for elk, not to hunt them, just to see what was there. We rode past Bearway Meadow and up into the hills as far as the satellite station on the top of Flock Mountain. Phil had no qualms about pushing his horse straight up the steep hills and coming off mudslides that scared me to death.

"Anyway, on that Sunday, Phil loaded Flirt in his homemade one-horse trailer and I wasn't at all sure that old trailer would hold together to get them to the Fopiano. I said something about my misgivings and Phil laughed, told me not to worry. When he pulled away, he was still grinning. He waved. That was the last time I saw him.

"I heard Phil was missing when Justin's wife, Shelli, called me at work about 10 o'clock on Wednesday morning. She said she was hesitant about calling because she didn't want to step on anybody's toes, Mom's toes to be specific. You have to know this about my mom. One time Justin had gotten thrown off a horse at Zack Keys' place near Richmond and ruptured his spleen. That can be a fatal injury. He was transported to Prineville and luckily they were able to save his life. But Mom never notified any of us. Finally Grandma Parton called and said Justin was in the hospital. That's the thing about Mom, she never wanted to worry any of us unnecessarily.

"Shelli asked if Mom had called me and I could tell from the tone of her voice something serious had happened. I said no and asked what was going on. Shelli said Phil had gone for a ride on my filly and had never returned. When she said that, I felt this god-awful wave of coldness wash over me. I turned to the girl I worked with at Jefferson County Title Company— she was the one who had sold me Flirt—and I said, 'My brother took Flirt for a ride and he never came home.'"

11

"She said, 'Don't worry. He'll be okay.'

"I told her, 'No he won't.' That was my gut feeling; something bad had happened to Phil. I told my boss I was taking the day off and I headed home. My plan was to load a horse, drive to Mitchell and search until I found Phil. I called my husband, told him what I was going to do and he said to wait, that he wanted to go with me. I loaded our horses, made arrangements for someone to come and stay with the kids when they got home from school, and Bill and I took off for Mitchell.

"As we traveled I kept seeing Phil in my mind; sitting on the tailgate of his pickup truck, drinking a beer and giving everyone a bad time for overreacting. We reached the Fopiano and Phil was not there. There were a lot of rigs and horse trailers but nobody was around, they were all out searching. We were in the process of dropping the horses when Mom and my stepdad arrived. Jim wasted no time in saying he figured that flighty little filly of mine had gone down and Phil was trapped out there somewhere, too injured to make it home on his own.

"When he said that I felt guilty, as if I was the one responsible for Phil's disappearance. I recalled a girlfriend of mine from Mitchell who had a horse go down with her, and if someone hadn't been there to pull the horse off, the horse would have flailed around and killed her. If a horse can't get his head up, he'll die trying. I was afraid Flirt had done that, gone down with Phil, and I knew if that's what happened I could never forgive myself.

"Jim, Bill and I rode to the gates closest to the barn, looking for any sign. Flirt had been shod for the first time just the week before and her shoes were heart shaped, and triple ought. They were very distinctive, and once we saw them, up above the cemetery, we knew we were on the right trail. Phil wandered here and there. He never was the type to stay on roads or even trails. Phil went where Phil wanted to go. He was not easy to follow. The days had been hot and dry and the nights cold. The ground was hard-packed and dusty. We rode all that afternoon until it started to get dark. We heard human voices, then a dog barking, and I told Bill, 'That's Poncho! That's Phil's dog.'

"I spurred my horse into a high lope, following an old skid trail, and within a couple minutes came upon Jimmy Collins and Pat Perry. Poncho was there, barking, yipping and carrying on. He was only 6 months old and was definitely acting like a silly puppy.

"They told me Justin was around the hill, following horse tracks, that the horse was probably nearby. I said I had to let Justin know Poncho had been found. When I caught up with Justin I told him the news and he said Phil had to be near where the dog was found. He rode in that direction. Bill and I decided to circle around. We climbed to a bench and split up in order to cover more territory. By then it was nearly dark. I followed along a game trail headed west, and as I came through a little draw I looked and there was Flirt standing beside a boulder. I called to Bill, "I see Flirt!"

"Bill rode toward me. As it turned out, if I hadn't diverted him, if he had continued on, he would have found Phil. I talked to Flirt as I rode forward, trying to keep any emotion out of my voice. Her head came up and she looked in my direction. She had a snaffle bit in her mouth, no reins, and the lead rope was tied around her neck. That was the way Phil always rode. The rope was maybe 15 feet long. Flirt's eyes were big and I knew she was scared. She snorted as we approached. I leaned in the saddle and grabbed the lead rope. When it came tight, Flirt reared and went over backwards. She didn't want any pressure put on her. I dropped the rope and tried to reassure her, saying, 'It's okay, baby. I'm not going to hurt you.'

"Once again I took the lead rope, and this time Flirt recognized me and responded; she sucked up against my horse so tight she dang near knocked me out of the saddle. I checked to see if she was hurt. Her front legs were a little skinned, and that was about it, a few cuts and a little dried blood, nothing serious. The cinch was tight and the saddle unmarked. There was no evidence to suggest a struggle. It was as though Phil had simply stepped off Flirt and turned her loose.

"I hollered to Justin that I had found Flirt. He was close enough that he came immediately. I told him I wanted to go back to the ranch and tell Mom we had found Poncho and Flirt. He told me how to go, to follow the fence line to the road and the road would empty out just above the cemetery. He said he would keep looking for Phil until he found him."

As Tina rode in the direction of the ranch the moon slipped over the bald hills on the far side of Waterman Flat and bathed the countryside in a soft, white light. She rode in silence, listening to the horses shuffling their feet on the dry hollow ground, deer bounding away, elk mewing and owls calling back and forth with their lonesome voices spilling out across the land. Several times Flirt crowded so close she caused Tina's mount to stumble and Tina thought, if Flirt could only talk and tell what had happened to Phil, and where he could be found, then all her burning questions would be answered. As Tina drew near the ranch, her apprehension built to dread and now she suddenly did not want to face her mother.

"The moon was so bright it was almost like day," recalled Tina. "I came off the ridge and hit the road and I was thinking about parades I had attended where someone led a riderless horse to symbolize the death of a cowboy. That is always so sad. But me, leading Flirt down the road, I knew it was the exact same thing.

"I saw her running toward me—Mom—and when she drew near she wailed, 'Where is he? Where's Phil?' And to me, seeing the moonlight on Mom's face and the tears wet on her cheeks, that was the most awful moment of my life. I felt the weight of her grief, as well as my own.

"I found myself saying, "I don't know where he is, but I found Flirt, and Poncho came down. Phil has to be somewhere close. Justin will find him.'"

Wendy appeared. She took Flirt and Tina's horse to the barn to unsaddle them. Tina walked with an arm slung around her mother's shoulders, and when they reached the house they sat in the semi-darkness and waited for someone to come, for someone to tell them they had found Phil. Time dragged by ever so slowly. Every minute seemed like an hour. Tina listened to the sounds of her mother's ragged breathing, to Georgia's too, and tried to make sure they couldn't hear her breathing. She wondered if they could.

⊕ ⊕ ⊕

An old man sat in the dim shadows on the white bench in front of the Wheeler County Trading Post in downtown Mitchell. He gingerly held a cigarette between nicotine stained fingers and blew a cloud of blue smoke into the moonlit night. A passerby paused to ask what the latest development was in the ongoing search for the lost cowboy. The old man took a contemplative puff and replied, "Ain't ya heard, they done found the dog and the horse, too. Said there was blood on the saddle. The kid must 'ave got shot off his horse. Damn pity is what it is."

⊕ ⊕ ⊕

Headlights played across the dark interior of the ranch house, and after a moment or two, members of the Wheeler County Search and Rescue began to drift inside. They refused the coffee that was offered and said they wanted to start searching immediately. Tina told them about finding the horse and the dog and they asked if she could lead them to the area. Tina said yes. She was thankful they had come and wanted to get away, leave the brooding people in the house and return to where she might do something constructive to further the search.

One man stayed behind at the ranch house to run the base radio, while the others drove to the ridge near Bearway Meadow. Here the team divided into two groups, one went up the ridge and the other followed the skid trail along the fence line dividing the Fopiano from the adjoining Sixshooter Ranch. Tina joined the first group because it included several men who worked with her stepfather on the Oregon State Highway Department crew.

"The searchers were wearing hats and coats and had food and water in their packs," said Tina. "They were prepared to stay the night. I led them to where I found Flirt and they started backtracking. I was amazed how they were able to track at night. By laying a flashlight on a track, and pointing it in the direction the tracks were headed, it was almost like magic the way the next track was revealed. Even when the trail passed over a bed of pine needles the tracking was easy because pine needles have a shiny side from where they have been in contact with the sun and weather, and a dull side underneath. When pine needles are stepped on they generally roll. The dull marks in the sheen of a bed of pine needles can be followed almost at a trot.

"If we only had Flirt's tracks to follow, it would have been easy, but by that time there had been so many horses and people through there searching that we kept getting sidetracked, following wrong leads. It was impossible to stay on a single set of tracks and finally we gave up, turned off our flashlights, and wandered around in the moonlight calling Phil's name.

"At one point, on the hill opposite from where I had found Flirt, I saw a light, and whoever was using the light seemed to be looking for something in a small area. I flipped on my flashlight, shined it in the direction of the other flashlight, and hollered, 'Hey! Who's over there?'

"Immediately the light was turned off. That struck me as very odd. I knew where the members of our group were, and from radio contact knew the second group had worked their way back toward the ranch and were several miles east of us. Who was that on the other hill, at midnight, and what was that person searching for? Certainly not trying to find Phil. That puzzled me at the time, and it puzzles me still.

"Finally I announced I was going to go back to the ranch and try to get a couple hours of sleep. They asked if I knew how to get there. I assured them I did. I walked for a couple miles, was almost to the road, when a man's voice startled me,

'Who goes there?' A figure stepped from the shadows of a pine tree and into the moonlight. I recognized Dave Humphries. I had grown up with Dave, gone to school with him. He was out there in the night with no warm jacket, no flashlight, nothing. I asked him what he was doing.

"'Heading back,' he told me. 'My rig's over there. Wanna lift?'

"I said I did, and we walked and talked and Dave told me one thing that stuck with me. He said, because of the amount of time that had passed, he figured Phil was injured and had probably dragged himself to a place where he could stay out of the sun during the heat of the day, and yet pile leaves and whatnot on him to stay warm during the cold of the night. When I questioned him about this, he said the searchers should be looking around windfalls, and that Phil would be hard to find. At the time, his statement was very disturbing to me.

"Later I learned Dave had run into a bow hunter that day, surprised the guy down by the lake, but he never mentioned anything to me about the incident. I've never seen Dave again to ask him why not, why he didn't tell me.

"Dave dropped me off at the house and I went inside and joined Mom, Wendy, Shelli and Georgia. They were seated around the kitchen table. One of the searchers came in, had a cup of coffee and happened to mention Sandy Edgeman had run into a bow hunter and the bow hunter drew down on her. I was watching the others at the table and saw the way the blood seemed to drain from their faces, as it did mine I'm sure. It was the last week of bow season and even though bow hunting was not allowed on the Fopiano, a trespasser could have been there. I'm sure we all thought the same—that Phil had been shot by a bow hunter—but none of us voiced our fears."

⊕ ⊕ ⊕

"Did you hear, a bow hunter shot Phil, dug a hole and hid his body? That's the reason nobody's been able to find him."

⊕ ⊕ ⊕

The Warm Springs Search and Rescue tracking team, headed by Keith Baker and Stoney Miller, arrived from the Warm Springs Indian Reservation. After sleeping for an hour or two in their rigs, they made their way inside the ranch house. People were already gathering there and Georgia, Joyce, Wendy, Shelli and Tina were busy pouring coffee and fixing breakfast. A quad map was laid out across the kitchen table and members of the tracking team, and other searchers, filled their plates with ham, hash brown potatoes and eggs. They stood near the table eating as Sheriff Otho Caldera pointed to areas that had been searched. He finally tapped the map with an index finger and said, "Right here is where Phil's dog came down. And here is where the horse was found."

"When Otho told us that, I knew where we needed to concentrate our search," said Keith Baker. "In most cases, a dog will stick pretty close, even if its master has been hurt or is dead."

Searchers find it helpful to have some basic information on a subject, and while they waited for morning light, Keith and Stoney asked general questions about Phil—his height, weight, what he did for a living, what he had been wearing when he disappeared, and whether he was left or right-handed. Usually a person who becomes lost or disoriented, if he, or she, is right-handed that person circles to the left and a left-handed person circles to the right. Age matters because older people will most often venture into open country to increase their odds of being seen, while a young person invariably climbs uphill and hunkers in a thicket or beside a log because of their lingering womb instincts.

Although, because of the presence of the Brooks family, people were guarded about what they had to say, it was revealed Phil loved animals, was a proficient horseman, had trouble in school because he suffered from dyslexia, liked women and when he drank he sometimes drank to excess and could become rowdy. He was like a lot of men his age growing up in a rural environment. But probably the most vital piece of information concerned the horse Phil had been riding when he disappeared: its size, temperament, and most of all the distinctive, heart shaped triple ought shoes.

Keith Baker was the only white man on the otherwise all-Indian tracking crew from the Warm Springs Reservation. He was a big man, close to 6 feet, and 230 pounds. He was a veteran of two tours in Vietnam where he served as a sniper. His graying hair was gathered into a tight braid that fell down the middle of his back. He sported a roadrunner tattoo on his beefy left bicep and claimed he got into tracking and white-water rescue because, after having taken so many lives during the war, he felt he owed a debt to society. Now he wanted to try and save lives. He wore a pack around his waist with the tools he needed for tracking, survival gear and a week's supply of rations.

That morning at breakfast, and during the briefing session, Keith met and observed the Brooks family members and was impressed at their unwavering spirit and belief that Phil would be found alive. He hoped he could find Phil in time, as he had found other lost hunters and rafters, but he was experienced enough to know that not every story has a happy ending. He prayed this one would.

"Pat Perry led the way," recalled Keith, "and what struck me as strange was that, on the drive in, we passed an open campfire and a lit lantern inside a tent. Back at the ranch we had been advised this was a remote area. I asked what this sign of civilization could possibly be and was informed, 'That's a hunting camp.' I pressed further and was told that Mike and Roetta Williams leased the hunting rights to the Collins' property and brought in fee hunters, mainly from California, and that they used the hunting camp as their base of operation. I wondered if anyone had talked to the Williams' to see if they might have any information about the missing cowboy, but I didn't press the issue."

Pat drove to the site where the dog had come off the hill, and where the horse had been found. The trackers got out of their rigs. The air was cool and the dawning of a new day was beginning to sweeten the sky with gray light. As they hiked across a flat and through a shallow gully, Bearway Meadow was off to their left, north, and as they moved toward higher ground a Caterpillar could be heard starting up, first the gas engine and then the slow pop-pop-pop of the diesel engine firing. It was at least a mile away, on the far side of Bearway Meadow, and Keith made a mental note of it, figuring if someone was in the vicinity, logging or building roads, maybe one of those workers had seen or heard something. Ahead was a forested area, logged maybe 15 or 20 years before, and there were thick clusters of small trees that had never been thinned. The team of trackers spread out and began a grid sweep up a narrow, timbered draw, looking for tracks or any physical evidence, from candy wrappers to cigarette butts, and of course they were looking for an injured cowboy, or a body.

"I was on the far left wing," said Keith. "Had gone only a few dozen steps, when I noticed the ground at my feet had been disturbed. Looking more closely, and even though the light was not real good, I clearly recognized the print of a horseshoe—very small, heart shaped—and instinctively knew this was the track from Phil's horse. The prints were dug in deep, side-by-side, indicating the horse was bounding, moving fast and planting its feet hard. When I looked up the rocky spine in front of me, I saw more tracks, evenly spaced, and even farther up the hill I spotted a foreign object. It wasn't anything I could immediately recognize or identify; it was just something that shouldn't have been there. To gain a vantage, I stepped onto a nearby rock and from there plainly saw a body on the ground, lying face up. Definitely male.

"'I have a body,' I called downhill, and then waited until Stoney Miller worked his way to me. He marked where I was standing with red ribbon and I eased forward. As I approached the body I looked for any signs of movement; there were none. The right leg was bent at the knee and slightly elevated, left leg at full extension, dried blood on shirt mid-torso, left of center, but not a lot of blood, left hand extended out and down, cowboy hat pushed back cradling his head, face fully exposed.

The skin was pale, almost translucent and slightly blue tinged. The eyes were open, glazed over, and although the birds and animals hadn't bothered him, there were insects at the mouth and nose. Positively, the subject was dead. I made mental note of the broken limbs near the body, and the tracks of the horse leaving the area. It appeared the horse had been spooked, and my initial judgment was the horse had run the subject, which I assumed was Phil Brooks, into a limb and that was what killed him.

"I backtracked, marking each step out with a ribbon. Upon reaching Stoney, and not wanting to alert everyone to the fact Phil was dead, I tried to reach Otho on the radio to inform him of our discovery. He apparently was not within range, but after a moment he responded. I purposely tried to be vague and said we needed to talk. He wanted to know what was going on. Again I told him we needed to talk. He still wasn't catching on and asked if we had found something. One of the people from law enforcement said to say we had a 10-7, which I guess meant we had a body. I repeated those words and Otho replied, 'Headed that way. Be there in a minute.'"

The tracking crew strung orange ribbon from tree to tree, marking off the area in an attempt to preserve it. A number of horseback riders approached and Keith turned them away, saying he couldn't let them pass. They wanted to know why and Keith told them the sheriff had requested this area be preserved as a search site. One of the riders tried to go up and around, and Stoney sent a member of the tracking crew to head him off.

Otho arrived and Keith led him to the hill and told him to walk on the ribbons. Keith followed behind. As they approached the body Otho confirmed it was Phil Brooks and he stood for a long moment, hesitant to investigate any further; and then he bent, reached with his right hand and pulled back the shirt to expose the chest area. There was an entrance wound—a round, perfectly symmetrical, purple dot—over the heart and Otho jerked his hand away, straightened and exclaimed, "He's been shot. We have a homicide!"

Otho looked around to see from which direction the shot might have been fired. Phil's body was in a very small opening in a thick tangle of trees. There were only three possible places from which a shooter could have seen into this area. One was from Bearway Meadow, but he quickly dismissed this option because it would have required a shot in excess of a thousand yards. Another was downhill, less than 100 yards at the base of the rocky ridge, and the third was across the way, on the opposite hill, a distance of nearly 400 yards. Otho reasoned, if the shot came from the shorter distance, then the shooter had definitely seen Phil and it was most likely a cold-blooded murder. But if it was the longer shot, Otho reasoned the shooter could possibly have mistaken the horse for an elk.

Otho, who had been the Wheeler County sheriff for 21 years, mulled over a wide range of considerations and made a snap decision. In part his decision was based on the fact Wheeler County was strapped for funding and could not afford the expense of a major homicide investigation—the first homicide in the county since 1935—but also included in the mix was the fact Otho had never investigated a murder and personally lacked a background in law enforcement. He had won election after election because he was a hard-nosed man who saw law and order as black and white. He was popular with voters. Everyone knew Otho and he was universally respected. What folks did not know was that Otho had recently been diagnosed with multiple sclerosis. He was taking medication and had suffered from involuntary muscle twitching, occasional blurred vision and some short-term memory loss. Based on these considerations, Otho decided to turn the investigation over to the Oregon State Police.

⊕ ⊕ ⊕

"The trackers worked the area pretty hard," recalled Pat Perry, "and all the while Phil's body laid up there on the ridge. I hated to see that because, although it was cold at night, the daytime temperatures were running into the 90s. I didn't want the body to deteriorate any more than it already had and asked Otho if I could cover Phil with a blanket. At first he refused, but later he said he figured it would be all right. I got a blanket from one of the horsemen. They were still being held at the base of the hill. Nobody had bothered to tell them a body had been located. Jim and Justin Brooks were in the group. I felt bad for them, that they didn't know, but I had been warned not to shoot off my mouth and I didn't.

"When I returned with the blanket, Otho was rolling the body to one side, looking for an exit wound. There was none, and that was a pretty good indication the bullet was still inside. I hoped it would be in good enough shape for ballistic tests, and useful as evidence to hang the guilty party. I asked Otho if he had called the coroner. He acted confused, said he hadn't. I knew how long it'd take for the coroner to get all the way out to the ranch and I jumped Otho's ass. He told me he'd take care of it.

"Two state policemen arrived. The one standing nearest to the body wanted to know if I had a pocketknife. I told him, 'Yeah, I got a pocketknife.' He asked to borrow it. I said, 'What do you want it for?' He said he was going to collect tissue from around the bullet hole as evidence. I told him, 'Not with my knife you won't.' He borrowed a knife from someone else, and I watched him place the sample in a plastic bag.

"After that I went to talk to Jim Brooks—knowing that by then he had been told Phil was dead—and I asked if he had a preference on which mortuary to call. He was in shock and told me, 'Pat, do whatever you think is best.' I used a mobile phone and called the Prineville Funeral Home, told them to come pick up the body and gave directions on how to get to the Fopiano."

The state police officers had informed the riders congregated at the base of the hill that they had recovered the body and there was no reason for them to hang around. They advised the riders to go home. Then they told the trackers the state police investigative team was attending a meeting in Salem and would not arrive on site until late in the afternoon.

The trackers, within view of the body, ate lunch while the Wheeler County deputies took their statements.

After eating, Keith Baker asked Otho for permission to backtrack Phil, and although the state police officers protested, Otho said he was still in charge of the investigation and gave his permission. Keith and his tracking partner, Vinson Macy, a Warm Springs Indian, followed the tracks uphill from Phil's body. They moved slowly, sometimes on their hands and knees, using tracking sticks to measure distances, marking each footprint and hoof print with red ribbons, trying to read and interpret what the sign meant.

⊕ ⊕ ⊕

Tina was in the saddle, riding in the dark, and as the twinkling stars faded and the soft hues of morning seeped into the eastern sky, she remembered what Dave Humphries had told her the night before and she searched behind rocks, windfalls and brush piles. She puzzled over why, if Phil had been injured, he had not built a fire. Phil smoked hand-rolled cigarettes and she knew he would have matches with him. A fire would keep him warm at night and a fire would signal his location to the searchers. When Tina came across Justin, who had spent the night in the woods just sitting on a high point and trying to think where his brother might be, she asked him why Phil had not started a fire.

"Jimmy Collins don't want nobody smoking. The woods are tinder dry and he's afraid of forest fires," responded Justin. He went on to say that whenever Phil was going into the backcountry, he always left behind his cigarettes and matches and took a can of chew to feed his nicotine habit.

"I kept searching the area but as I drew near to where I had found the horse, I was turned back by law enforcement," said Tina. "A number of riders came to that point, and we were all forced to wait there together. Finally a state police officer came and told us Phil's body had been found. We were directed to return to the ranch.

"When I came off the ridge and looked out over all the rigs parked there, knew how many friends had come to help out in the search, I felt overwhelmed with emotions. People, horses and dogs were everywhere. When I rode in, I didn't want to see anyone, talk to anyone, and rode to our horse trailer and tried to hide there. Bill found me. We talked and I knew I had to be with Mom. I leaned on Bill and we started for the house.

"On the way, I spotted Shelli, Justin's wife, lying on the ground near the fence, curled in a fetal position, legs drawn up, with blankets and coats piled over her. A friend was standing nearby. I didn't figure there was anything I could do—she was in shock—and I went inside. I saw Wendy and she was falling apart and then Pat Perry found me, put his arms around me and said he wished he could have done more. I said, 'I know.' Then he kissed my cheek and left me alone."

Justin and his father were standing in the yard, but not together. Linda Keys was with Joyce. It seemed as though the family was purposefully staying away from each other. Maybe their thinking was, if they were not together, they didn't have to talk about, or deal with Phil's death.

Many of the searchers had brought food with them, and as if this were a giant neighborhood potluck, the food was arranged on long tables in the yard. As the searchers drifted in, some grabbed a bite to eat and others just poured themselves a cup of coffee. Mostly people stood around, saying very little, waiting for someone to tell them something.

A group from law enforcement arrived, including the two state police officers dressed in crisp, blue uniforms, Tom Cutsforth, the Wheeler County District Attorney, Sheriff Otho Caldera and Deputy Craig Ward, as well as two Reserve Deputies, Dave Rouse and Jim Walker. They stepped inside the house and after a few minutes, Linda Keys was asked to join them. A few more minutes passed and then one of the state troopers opened the door and requested all immediate members of the Brooks family to please step inside.

"I don't know how Linda was chosen to deliver the news," said Tina. "I suppose it was because she was the Wheeler County Justice of the Peace and a close friend of our family."

After the family was gathered in the living room, Linda stepped forward and said, "I don't know how to tell you what it is I have to tell you…" She faltered.

Jim Brooks spoke up, "Damn it, don't beat around the bush. Say what you gotta say. Give it to us straight out."

Linda took a deep breath. "Phil was shot."

"Oh, Jesus!" Justin cried out, and took a step back. Jim never uttered a word but he looked as though he had taken a hard punch to the pit of his stomach and bent slightly at the waist. Joyce's expression did not change. It was as blank as a white wall. Tina gave an audible sigh.

"To me it seemed as though that black cloud that had been hovering over my head was finally gone," said Tina. "All the time I had been blaming myself, and blaming my horse, and now we had been told some person had shot Phil. I never considered the ramifications of that; what I experienced was this tremendous sense of relief. It had not been my horse that killed Phil."

Linda continued to talk, saying if they had found Phil earlier, there was nothing any of them could have done, that Phil died instantly on Tuesday afternoon. Tina and Justin, relieved Phil had not suffered, exchanged looks, then nods.

"What was he shot with?" Jim wanted to know.

"We're not certain but we believe it was a small caliber at close range," said Linda and added, "Maybe he confronted a trespasser. We don't know."

Deputy Craig Ward stepped forward and told the family what they had just learned—that Phil had been shot—was strictly confidential and he went on to threaten, "If you tell someone, anyone at all, you risk being arrested for hindering prosecution."

Tina spoke up and said, since Jimmy and Georgia Collins owned the ranch and were like family, they should be told. Jimmy responded by recoiling and saying, "He was shot? Holy shit!" Georgia—Phil had been like a son to her—cried and kept repeating, "No, not on the Fopiano. No way. Not on the Fopiano."

Craig announced the meeting was over and suggested the family leave the investigation to the authorities and go home. Tina asked about Phil, when the body would be released. Craig said it would not be any time soon, that in the case of a homicide, an autopsy was required and it would take several days. Then Tina asked if they needed Flirt. Craig turned to Otho. Otho shook his head. Craig said, "Take her home."

"I went outside to load my horse," said Tina. "I thought I was handling things pretty well, but when I went to get Flirt's halter from Phil's pickup, I opened the door and the sadness of losing Phil, having him shot, just hit me. His hand had touched the door handle I was touching. The inside smelled like Phil. He had breathed the same air I was breathing. His cigarette papers, tobacco and matches were on the seat. I lost it, started sobbing and my legs went wobbly. I leaned against the side of the pickup and slumped down to where one knee was touching the ground."

A state policeman took hold of Tina by the arm and lifted her. He pulled her a few steps away from the pickup while another officer wrapped yellow plastic ribbon with the words "CRIME SCENE" printed on it in bold letters, around the pickup. The policeman holding Tina said, "There could be evidence there. Stay away." He released her, and to make his point he gave her a little shove.

Tina was taken aback. She was unsure how to react, whether to fight or simply go along with the authorities because, after all, they had a job to do—find the person responsible for killing Phil.

Flirt was loaded in the horse trailer along with Bill and Tina's other two horses. As they pulled away from the ranch Bill shook his head and said, "Tell me, why would someone want to shoot Phil?"

"When he said that—this is really bizarre—but I saw a bright light, as bright as if I was staring into the sun," said Tina. "In that yellow ball appeared a vision of Phil, a silhouette of him with the light shining through. It was from his neck up; he had on a cowboy hat and was wearing this crooked smile he'd get whenever something amused him. He looked happy, content, at ease."

Tina was at a loss to explain why this vision of Phil had appeared to her. There was an 11 year age difference between Phil and Tina. He was her stepbrother and according to Tina, "We were close, but never really close-close." She was afraid maybe the grief was causing her to go crazy and that night, when she closed her eyes, the vision remained—Phil's face drifting in the black void, yellowish gray light in a halo around him, light leaking through his crooked smile. For three full days and nights the vision remained, as if indelibly imprinted on her eyes and then it went away and never returned.

⊕ ⊕ ⊕

Although the investigation was halted awaiting the arrival of the state police investigative team, Sheriff Otho Caldera gave Keith Baker and Vinson Macy permission to backtrack Phil and the horse. Keith related, "What we learned from the backtracking we were allowed to do, is that about a half-mile above where Phil was killed, on a bench with a well-worn game trail leading through the middle of it, Phil's horse was running flat out. What made that horse run hard? I don't know because we were not allowed to backtrack above that point. What I do know is that at the upper point of our search, Phil's horse leaped a windfall a couple of feet high. The horse did not go around the obstruction and that is abnormal. But what does it mean? I don't make assumptions but common sense dictates it could mean one of two things; the horse was either being pushed by the rider to do something it wasn't comfortable doing, or it was scared and running away.

"Phil did not have control of the horse, and in fact he lost a rein while the horse was running. The horse stepped on it, broke it off. We found the rein and that's also a very odd occurrence, for a cowboy as experienced Phil was, to lose a rein. The sign revealed, after losing the rein, the horse continued running and was out of control until Phil cranked on his one remaining rein, the right one, and brought the horse's head around, causing the horse to veer to the right and side-step. A horse can't do much when its head is pulled back to the rider's knees. At that point Phil had regained control, and yet he didn't stop, he kept going for another hundred yards. Then he finally brought the horse to an abrupt, sliding stop. He dismounted; most likely he jerry-rigged the rein, but I don't know that for a fact. I do know he cleared away the pine needles and duff with the sole of his right boot, down to bare dirt, and with his heel drew a straight line and an arrow pointing uphill, in the direction of where we found the rein. Then he remounted, started down off the hill in the direction of the skid trail, abruptly changed his mind and rode onto the rocky ridge. Phil got off his horse and led it 26.8 feet to where he was killed.

"Those are the details I know as fact. I had tracked Phil around the hill on the skid trail, and I had tracked him on the bench above, down to where he was killed. What I wanted to know was what happened between those two points—from the skid trail to where I picked up his track again on the bench. To me, that was the key. Something, or someone, diverted him from his intended route. He had been returning to the ranch, and it would have taken him less than a half hour to get there. It was getting late in the day, after 5 o'clock. His horse was tired and was slowing down. But for some reason, and it had to be something substantial, Phil turned straight up the hill from the skid trail. Why? Did a cougar scream, a bear growl, an elk bugle? Did he hear a shot? Did he hear someone? Did a hunter blow an elk call? What was it?

"And when I had the answer to what turned him up the hill then I wanted to know what happened on top. I believe something, or someone, threatened Phil and the horse. Threatened them to the point they wanted to put distance between them and the perceived threat. I say that for a number of reasons: the horse was running wild and jumped a windfall; Phil lost a rein and yet waited to get control of the horse; he regained control but kept going. He stopped, got off the horse, but rather than go back and get the rein, he drew an arrow to the spot and continued on. That tells me he did not feel comfortable about going back. And then, of course, I wanted to know why he chose to go to the point where he was killed. That spot does afford some protection, to a limited degree, but more than anything it offers a view of the game trail through the bottom of the draw, as well as the road leading to Bearway Meadow. It is a very logical choice if Phil had wanted to observe a specific area, thinking something, or someone, might pass along the game trail or the road.

"There were answers to at least some of those questions in the dirt and I could have found them, but the state police never allowed me to find the missing pieces, fit them together and complete the puzzle. They were impatient and thought Vinson and I were taking too much time following the sign. We were told to stop and await the arrival of the investigative team. I can't help but think the case would have been solved, and the killer's identity revealed, if only we had been allowed to continue tracking that first day."

⊕ ⊕ ⊕

As the sheriff of Wheeler County, Otho was still officially the man in charge of the Phil Brooks homicide investigation. But as that first long day wore on Otho had his deputy, Craig Ward, take an active role in talking to the media. Reporters from the *Oregonian*, Eugene *Register-Guard*, Bend *Bulletin*, and the Prineville *Central Oregonian* wanted information and Channel 21, the local television station from Bend, as well as several television stations from Portland, requested interviews. The shooting death of a cowboy was big news, but Craig Ward had good reason to be uneasy in the glare of the media spotlight. He knew it was only a matter of time before an inquisitive reporter, or television personality, recognized his name and put two-and-two together.

Craig Ward was a tall man, thin, and he liked to dress like a western gunslinger; wearing snakeskin cowboy boots with tight black pants tucked in the hand-tooled tops, a double-breasted shirt and a flat-brimmed cowboy hat. He lived up in the hills 18 miles from the Wheeler County seat of Fossil, in a rustic 700 square foot cabin; a family of five living without running water, electricity, telephone or television. Some of Craig's neighbors claimed the deputy practiced quick-draw, and at any time of the day or night the sound of shots could be heard. They said the constant shooting was unnerving.

"Not everybody got along with Craig," claimed Jeanie Perry. "He used to be a police officer in Portland before he came here and he wore two crosses pinned on his shirt right next to his shiny badge. He claimed the crosses represented the two people he shot in the line of duty. Some folks thought it was terrible to advertise such a thing, like he was proud he had killed someone."

One of the shootings occurred in 1985, when Craig shot a robber who had taken a hostage, and two years later Craig killed a troubled teenage boy who was threatening a family member. After the second shooting, Craig claimed a stress related disability and he said of that time, "I was pretty much a basket case, dysfunctional and arguably dangerous. When I realized I wanted to go out in a blaze of glory, wanted to die, I knew it was time to get out. We moved to Wheeler County which is about as isolated as I could be. How much further away can you get than a place that does not have a traffic light within a hundred miles?"

The shootings in the line of duty, ruled justifiable, were one thing, but Craig had more skeletons in the closet. And what made him most uncomfortable when dealing with the media was an incident that had occurred in April 1981. He was a Portland police officer, working the Northeast Precinct, and along with his partner, Jimmy Galloway, Craig had raced through alleyways in their patrol car to purposely run over possums. They gathered four dead possums and dumped them on the front steps of the Burger Barn, a business whose sign out front advertised *"soul food"* and was owned by an African-American. To the black and liberal communities, this stupid prank evoked an image of the Ku Klux Klan and a march was held in downtown Portland that ended on Oak Street in front of the police bureau. Protesters demanded that Charles Jordan, the black city commissioner in charge of the police bureau, fire the white officers involved in the possum-dumping incident. Politics prevailed and the officers were fired. This led to the Portland Police Union filing a grievance on behalf of their brother officers and holding a counter-demonstration with several hundred uniformed officers marching on city hall.

A hearing was held on the grievance and an arbitrator made his ruling, reinstating the officers with a mere slap on the wrist, giving them 30-day unpaid suspensions and directing the city to pay them for the remainder of the time they had not worked. The owner of the Burger Barn filed a $3.4 million civil-rights suit against the city, but eventually agreed to a $64,000 cash settlement.

When someone from the media did recognize Craig Ward's name, and quietly asked him about the possum-dumping incident, Craig hung his head in shame and replied, "That was the biggest mistake of my life. I put the city through hell and brought discredit to the bureau. But it wasn't done out of meanness or racial motivation. It's my fault, and I try to make amends for it every day."

⊕ ⊕ ⊕

Not until 5:30 p.m. did the state police investigative team, who had been attending a meeting in Salem, finally arrive at the site where Phil Brooks remained on the hillside under the blanket Pat Perry had laid over him to protect him from the flies. The state police came riding in like the cavalry to an Indian uprising.

"They were dressed like a bunch of city boys, wearing suits and ties and fancy slip on shoes," recalled Keith Baker. "They certainly weren't dressed to be out in the woods. When they tried to climb the hill to the body, their leather-soled, slick-bottomed shoes slipped on rocks and pine needles, and when they lost their footing they cussed and complained. If it hadn't of been such a serious situation, it would have been comical."

The state police quickly discovered the small opening in the trees where Phil had been found afforded only three opportunities from which a shot could have been fired. The first was from an extreme distance, coming from Bearway Meadow, and in excess of a thousand yards. Even though that was a remote possibility, the state police zeroed in on that scenario. Keith Baker showed them how Phil had been facing when he was killed, on his haunches, looking downhill. He said when Phil was shot he fell over backwards and to prove his point he showed the tracks in the dirt and pointed to the cowboy hat that remained on Phil's head. He said if Phil had been facing the meadow, the tracks would indicate that. They did not.

Of the two remaining options, one was across the way on the opposite hillside, a distance of approximately 400 yards. The other possibility was at the base of the rocky ridge, a distance of less than 100 yards. Those were the only windows in the maze of trees that would have been available to the shooter.

"The state police sent me and Vinson downhill to see if we could locate any sign of a shooter," said Keith. "Vinson cut sign first and called out. The first reaction by the state police was for everyone to freeze, but that was only momentary, and then they rushed Vinson. I called out, telling the officers to stay back and pleading with them to allow us to work the track. But when I went down to help Vinson, the state police crowded in so close around me that I had to tell them to step back and give me room. And they questioned me on everything I was doing. I tried to be patient, do my job and explain what I was finding, but it had been a long day. I was tired and a bit peeved.

"The tracks I was working revealed the person had been running, scrambling and trying to get away. The officers were standing behind me, with the sun at their backs and they couldn't see what I saw down low. Since they couldn't see it, or read the sign I was seeing, they insinuated I was fabricating evidence.

"In my defense, allow me to admit that I'm not always the world's most tactful man. And as further explanation, I have to offer that I have a buddy, a World War II veteran, whose favorite expression is, 'What, are you stupid?'

"So here I had these state police officers dressed up in their suits and ties and slip on shoes, ridiculing me and the evidence I was generating, and finally when one of them stated he didn't see what I was seeing, I blurted out, 'What, are you stupid?' That went over like a lead balloon. One cop in particular glared at me. I figured I was dead. Then a senior officer broke the ice and asked my name. I told him. The senior officer chuckled and said, 'Mr. Baker, we don't know anything. Would you please teach us to read sign?'

"I am well aware that much of the world is asphalt and concrete and tracking is a dying art form. But I've tried to pass on my skills to others and have even taught tracking to kids. That was how I approached it with the state police, from square one, as if they were children. Using my tracking stick I pointed to specific areas of an individual track and showed how to use the angle of the sun to best see the depressions and ridges. A few of the officers caught on. They got down beside me and studied the sign. Some did not. They hung back and remained skeptical.

"I backtracked the subject to a point where this person had gone into a shooter's stance with one knee on the ground beside a tree. On this tree was a mark where the bark had been damaged. I pointed this out and a state policeman asked, 'Was it made by a rifle?'

"My response was that, in order to answer such a question would require conjecture on my part. I said, 'I don't make assumptions. I point out physical evidence. It's up to you to interpret that evidence. What I can tell you is this; someone leaned a hard object against this tree and damaged the bark. Now, it could have been a tracking stick, the counter weight on a bow, a rifle. I don't know. The other information I can determine from where the mark is located and the measurements I have taken is this person is approximately 5 feet 8 inches tall, weighs between 120 to 160 pounds, and if this was made by a rifle, the individual shoots right-handed.'

"The officers rushed me, basically they pushed me aside, and began searching around the tree, brushing away the duff, grass and dirt. I took a quick step back and said, 'Gentlemen, you're destroying this site.' I was informed they were looking for a brass casing and my continuing pleas to not further disturb the area fell on deaf ears. In the end, the officers found nothing, and the only remaining evidence at that vital location was the damaged bark on the tree. The state police destroyed everything else."

Not much daylight remained but Keith and Vinson were allowed to continue working the site. They discovered the possible shooter had smoked several cigarettes and then field striped the butts, leaving only tobacco. Then, after having assumed a shooter's stance, this person had reacted by jumping up, running several steps, trying to leap a dry wash, falling, scrambling and running some more. Near a big rock this person had stopped, leaned into the rock and pissed. The smell of urine was still evident.

"The state police made an assumption the subject had to have been a man and they wanted me to confirm it," said Keith. "I regret that I said it probably was a man, but in hindsight, I know it could have been a woman who stood close, or leaned against the rock and pissed like a man. Some women do that."

⊕ ⊕ ⊕

When the light began to fade, the state police finally agreed to release the body of Phil Brooks. Pat Perry, who had remained at the site all that long day, finally was able to place the body on the olive drab army stretcher, and with help, carry it downhill where it was loaded in the back of his pickup truck. Pat packed ice around the body to preserve it as much as possible, drove to the ranch and delivered the body to the hearse that had been sent from the Prineville Funeral Home.

⊕ ⊕ ⊕

The trackers and the state police worked until darkness prevailed. As they were driving the dirt road following Fopiano Creek, they met a pickup occupied by Mike and Roetta Williams. Detective Ringsage stopped the vehicle. He recognized Mike because they were friends and attended the same church. He informed Mike the area was part of a crime scene and was closed to all except law enforcement and authorized personnel. The Williams' turned around and followed the procession of vehicles, stopping when they reached their hunting camp. This chance meeting was never made note of in any of the police reports.

"When I inquired about the Williams' I was informed they had purchased the exclusive hunting rights on the Fopiano Ranch," recalled Keith Baker. "That was for rifle only. Bow hunting was not allowed. That night, when we met the Williams' on the road, it did seem very peculiar to me that someone would be coming into that area after dark. A reasonable person would question why, when there was no bow hunting allowed on the ranch and rifle season was several weeks away, anyone should be driving in there, especially at night. As far as I know, nobody ever asked the Williams' what business they had to be there that night."

⊕ ⊕ ⊕

The initial police report, as filed by lead Detective Robin F. Ringsage, described the victim, Phil Brooks, in graphic detail; all the way down to his slightly receding hairline, the white socks he was wearing, size 11D cowboy boots, his lack of underwear and noting the shirt with snagged sleeves had an entrance hole in the front, but no exit hole. Further, the horse Phil had been riding was described as, "just over 2 years old and was dark brown chestnut colored with a bright blaze going from the forehead to the nose."

Detective Ringsage's report read: "On Thursday, September 22, 1994 I was advised that a Wheeler County cowboy had been found shot on the Fopiano Ranch. Believed he was the victim of a homicide. I was requested to go to the Fopiano Ranch and assist Wheeler County Sheriff's Dept. with this investigation.

"I arrived at the Fopiano Ranch and met with Deputy Craig Ward and he said the victim was employed by the Fopiano Ranch as a ranch hand and he and Jimmy Collins had spent Tuesday morning, September 20th sorting stray cattle. Victim asked for and received permission to take the afternoon off to work with his sister's green broke horse. The victim was last seen by Jimmy Collins heading toward the ranch headquarters at approximately 2 p.m. where he had left the horse while going home for lunch. It was believed that he intended to be gone for approx. 2 hours. When the victim did not arrive for work the following morning Jimmy Collins became concerned and subsequently called another rancher to have his hands assist in a search. It is estimated that up to 200 persons conducted a search prior to notifying the Wheeler County Sheriff's Department.

"At 2:41 p.m., September 21, 1994 the Wheeler County Sheriff's Department was notified the victim was missing. They subsequently requested the assistance of the Warm Springs Search and Rescue trackers, as well as employing their own searchers. At approx. 7:15 a.m., Thursday, September 22, the victim was found on a ridge near Bearway Meadow on the Fopiano Ranch by members of the Warm Springs Search and

Rescue. Sheriff Otho Caldera, and deputies and reserve deputies of the Wheeler County Sheriff's Department, secured the crime scene. At approx. 5:30 p.m. I arrived at the crime scene. Present were Keith Baker, Vinson Macy, James Surface, all from the Warm Springs Search and Rescue, Pat Perry, Tom Cutsforth, Wheeler County District Attorney and Wheeler County Sheriff Otho Caldera, and his reserve deputy, David Rouse.

"The crime scene is on the Fopiano Ranch, a 33,000 acre ranch owned by the brothers Jimmy and Bob Collins. This portion of the ranch is in Wheeler County. The victim was found lying on his back on a rocky, wooded ridge running along the east edge of Bearway Meadow. The victim's cowboy hat was positioned in an upward position, tipped back at the base of the victim's head. His left arm was at his left side and right arm closer to his body with the right hand on the right hip. Victim's right leg was bent at the knee with the knee pointing left while the left leg was extended in a straight position. Located off to the victim's left, down an incline, was a can of Skoal. According to Keith Baker a rein was found NE of the victim's body, between the rein and the victim's body an arrow shaped mark that appeared to be pointing in the general direction of where the single rein was found indicated according to Baker that the victim had gotten off his horse and then remounted and further he stated there were disturbances in several locations and that just above where the victim was found there were signs indicating the victim was off the horse and leading it down the ridge. The single rein has been entered into evidence at the Bend OSP office and should be noted this rein has a horseshoe print indicating it might have been stepped on."

⊕ ⊕ ⊕

The morning of September 23rd an investigative briefing was held at the Cinnabar Restaurant in Prineville, the county seat of Crook County. Attending this meeting were members of law enforcement, as well as the tracking team from Warm Springs Search and Rescue. Detective Robin "Robb" Ringsage let it be known at this briefing that he was heading up the investigation. He was a short man, no more than 5 feet 7 inches tall, sporting a small mustache and built slender, like a long distance-runner.

Not everyone was impressed with Detective Ringsage. Some of his detractors claimed he had a "Napoleon complex" and that he tried to take his 6-ounce badge and use it to exert a ton of authority. Even members of law enforcement found him to be, at times, arrogant, overbearing and abrasive. One person involved in the murder case described him as being, "Like a banty rooster protecting a manure pile."

The Phil Brooks homicide investigation was the largest investigation Detective Ringsage had ever headed up, and before it was over, his Achilles' heel would be revealed; his tendency to focus on one scenario and one scenario only, and to try to make the evidence fit that tight focus, while excluding and ignoring all other possibilities.

"I distinctly remember," said Keith Baker, "after the meeting in Prineville, we drove the 70 miles to the Fopiano Ranch. I was a passenger in the fourth vehicle in the procession, and when we reached the Williams' hunting camp, which is located approximately halfway between the bone-gate turnoff from Waterman Flat and Bearway Meadow, we came to an unexpected stop. A man and woman were in the Williams' hunting camp and they stepped forward and approached the first vehicle, the one Detective Ringsage was driving. An extended conversation, lasting five or ten minutes, ensued. I watched the way the man leaned down to converse with Detective Ringsage, while the woman stayed back a step or two. It appeared the man and Detective Ringsage were well acquainted, and every so often the man laughed or made some gesture with his hands.

"After that conversation ended, we continued on, and as we passed the camp the man and the woman remained standing near the road, watching us. I noticed a third person standing inside a tent, peering out the open flap. I could not say whether this person was a man or a woman, a boy or a girl. All I know is that it was a human being."

That morning Detective Ringsage assigned Keith to track the person who had taken a shooter's stance at the bottom of the ridge, *the short shot*. The tracks were of a person who had run wildly from the scene, had slipped and fallen crossing a dry wash and had urinated against a rock. Keith learned this individual's normal walking stride measured 18½ inches between toe and heel, the tracks were made by someone who wore work boots—Packer and White make that type of boot—and this particular boot had a toe that narrowed, a raised heel and the sole was well worn and had distinctive crack marks. From the stride, the way this individual swung the right leg and placed that foot on the ground, it was apparent that at some point in the past, this person had suffered a serious injury to their upper right leg. This person had not been in the military, where soldiers are taught to elongate their stride. This person took short choppy steps. And this person was not raised in the city. Most people from the city are used to walking on pavement and their feet turn slightly outward. This person was raised in the country, was used to walking on dirt, and walked with a pigeon-toed gait.

Keith followed the trail and saw where the person had stepped up on a log and then down. A log provides perfect habitat for a rattlesnake to lie under. An experienced outdoor person would never step over a log and risk being bitten. And there were several times this person had stopped, faced toward the road, and then hurried on. The tracks led a half-mile to a brush pile, where limbs and wood debris from a logging operation in the past had been piled. The trail followed onto the brush pile and Keith found a spot where this person had leaned down and placed something on the ground, hiding it from view, and leaving behind in the soft earth, marks of four fingers and a palm print.

"I called Detective Ringsage's attention to what I had found," said Keith. "He asked if it was a rifle that had been placed there. I said I didn't know, but what I could say was this person I had followed had placed something in the brush pile, and then retrieved it at a later date. I would not commit myself to anything more."

The tracks moved off the brush pile and ended with the person getting into a full-sized vehicle. From where the vehicle was parked, it would be nearly impossible to see it from the road. Keith searched the ground to make sure there had not been a second person involved. He found no other human tracks, but what startled him was to discover distinctive horse tracks, triple ought, heart shaped. And by backtracking, he located where Phil Brooks had been riding on the skid trail, and where he had undoubtedly seen the parked vehicle and ridden off the trail to investigate. He had proceeded to within a dozen paces of the vehicle and then returned to the skid trail and went on his way. Keith said this discovery caused him to wonder if Phil, having seen the vehicle parked at the brush pile, had ridden around the hill for about a mile, and then gone uphill on the off chance he might encounter the person from the vehicle. Keith's other thought was that a second person was involved and they might have been dropped off and hiked into the area. Could this person have been picked up at another location? Had the driver, or a hiker, taken a shot at Phil? Keith knew none of the answers to these questions and it bothered him that he did not.

"By looking at the tire tracks I knew several things," said Keith. "The tires were nearly brand-new, and they were 15 inch Les Schwab Wild Country tires. I told Detective Ringsage. He was amazed and wanted to know if I had memorized every tire tread. I laughed and told him, 'No, I just bought the exact same set of tires for my pickup last week. This tread is identical to mine.'"

Another thing Keith discovered by following the tire tracks to the main road was that there was a rickety bridge, a couple of planks crossing Fopiano Creek, that were hard to see and dangerous to cross. The driver knew enough to avoid the crossing, choosing to go around the makeshift bridge and drive through the creek. It stood to reason the driver was knowledgeable of the area, and had passed that way before.

⊕ ⊕ ⊕

Phil Brooks' body was transported to Portland, and on September 24, 1994 the state medical examiner, Dr. Ed Wilson, conducted an autopsy. Present at the examination were Detective Ringsage, Lieutenant John Spilker from the Oregon State Police crime lab in Pendleton and Tom Cutsforth, the Wheeler County District Attorney. Detective Ringsage noted in his report: "The victim had a wad of moist, red chewing tobacco between his teeth and gum, fly eggs were in nostrils, lips and on back—entrance wound was located 56 3/8 inches above the heel, 1/4 inch right of the middle, 1/4 inch above the traverse nipple line, the bullet path traveled through the junction of the breastbone and right fourth rib, through the aorta, traveled through the left portion of the backbone and came to rest beneath the skin 55 1/4 inches above the heel— the bullet was recovered."

The bullet, although mushroomed on the end, was relatively intact toward the base. Ballistic testing was conducted and it was determined the bullet was a .284 caliber. The bullet retention was measured at 99.6 grains. The lands were .029-.032 and the grooves were .110-.122. A rifle capable of firing such a round included: .280 Remington, .284 Winchester or Savage, and 7MM Magnum manufactured by Alpine, Winchester, Remington, Sako, Savage, Weatherby, or Ruger.

⊕ ⊕ ⊕

The autopsy report revealed the .284 bullet that killed Phil Brooks hit him dead center in the chest—the location in the center of a target commonly known as the ten-X spot—and it had exploded his heart, ricocheted off his left shoulder blade and lodged in his spine just under the skin. This fact, that a high-powered rifle fired from a distance of less than 100 yards had not blown through Phil's body, caused Detective Ringsage and District Attorney Tom Cutsforth a great deal of consternation. They felt the only logical explanation was that the fatal shot had to have been fired from a longer distance. They began concentrating the investigation on the 400-yard shot, what they began calling *the long shot*.

"Detective Ringsage wanted me to look for sign on the opposite ridge," related Keith Baker. "It was an open, east facing hill and the ground was soft and loose. This made for easy tracking. What I found were five sets of human footprints. Two of those were quickly determined to be members of the search team, one set was unknown and wandered around never reaching a position where this person could have seen Phil on the opposite ridge. The last two sets of tracks were determined to be of a suspicious nature and I worked them carefully, anyway I did, once again, up to a particular point."

The tracks indicated two people had come down the side hill. One set of tracks was made by a fairly new set of hiking boots and the tread was very distinctive. The stride was long and unique with a slight out-pitch of the left foot. This person did a lot of hiking in the woods and based upon the length of stride and how far the track was pressed into the dirt, Keith estimated this person weighed between 140 and 170 pounds. The second set of tracks was also remarkably distinctive. This person wore older boots and there was a chunk of tread missing from the heel of the right boot. This person was much heavier, over 200 pounds, and was more used to walking on pavement than dirt. The left foot splayed out more than the right foot when this person walked.

A wrapper from an energy bar was found and it was assumed it came from one of the two individuals. Detective Ringsage chose to ignore it and did not collect it as evidence. Coming off the hill, the tracks paralleled each other, about 15 feet apart, to a point where one of the individuals had cautiously approached a weathered stump where this person assumed a shooter's stance, using the stump for a rest. The other person stood nearby. Both were facing the hill where Phil was shot.

"From the tracks, I could tell these two individuals left the area of the stump in more of a hurry than they were before," said Keith. "Were they running away? They didn't seem to be afraid. They only seemed to be moving with a purpose. Perhaps they were apprehensive about being out in the open. I don't know. All I can say is they were moving a little faster than they had been. And they walked to where a narrow tired vehicle had been parked. It could have been a small pickup. It could have been a car. The sign here was obliterated because so many people had been in the area, from searchers to law enforcement.

"Detective Ringsage wanted me to say these people had left in a vehicle. I told him I could not do that. There was just too much sign, too much confusion to try and reach a single logical conclusion. Then he wanted me to backtrack and see where the two people came from. And while I was doing that, a team came in and swept the area around the weathered stump, looking for spent casings. I was told they found brass but it was all old brass."

That afternoon, a laser-sighting team arrived with their sophisticated equipment. On the open hillside they set up a tripod and instruments at the weathered stump. Across the way another tripod and a box with a silver disk were positioned where Phil's body was located. An officer in a yellow raincoat assumed the position where Phil had been squatting, but he was not visible on the opposite ridge. Nor did the laser-sighting test penetrate the trees and branches. What the laser-sighting team proved was that it would have been nearly impossible for anyone to shoot Phil from the weathered stump. But that scientific evidence didn't seem to dissuade or discourage Detective Ringsage or Tom Cutsforth. They wanted to make *the long shot* work because it was easier to explain why the bullet from the high-powered rifle had not blown through the victim's body.

"I tried to enlighten law enforcement," said Keith, "to the fact poachers oftentimes use short load ammunition—hand-loading only about half the smokeless gunpowder that a factory load will carry—allowing the round to exit the rifle at a slower rate of speed, subsonic, and therefore the report is much quieter. The problem with a short load is it has killing power out to only about a hundred yards. Law enforcement refused to consider the possibility. They were not interested in my theories. They had their minds made up, it was *the long shot* that killed Phil and nothing I could say would persuade them otherwise."

Detective Ringsage had Keith and the other trackers backtrack the two individuals on *the long shot*. At one point the trackers came across bright red feathers, fletching from an arrow, and they called Detective Ringsage's attention to it. He ignored it, did not bag it as possible evidence, he simply walked away. Most likely he had already made up his mind the two individuals he was following were not bow hunters, they were rifle hunters, and one of them had killed Phil Brooks.

While the tracks were being backtracked from *the long shot*, members of the state police investigative team happened to stumble across a makeshift camp in a dry wash a half-mile northwest of the location of Williams' hunting camp. Recovered from the site were a sleeping bag in a blue and gray stuff bag, a rolled up air mattress, a black pack frame, a bag of Twinkies, cookie bars, a box of pop tarts, three breakfast bars, a cheese and cracker snack pack, one fruit pack, two open juice drinks, berry flavored, and a piece of wood with the words, "Go to Bike" scratched into the wood with a sharp object.

It was immediately assumed this was a bow hunter's camp. The mention of bow hunters caused someone to remember that a bow hunter had threatened a woman on horseback, one of the original searchers. And someone else remembered that another searcher had reported finding a bow hunter hiding near the lake and this hunter had been wearing camo and had his face painted.

"It was like an avalanche," recalled Keith. "All this information came pouring out about bow hunters. Things got hectic and Detective Ringsage pulled us off *the long shot* and had us tracking around the makeshift camp, then pulled us off to track down by the lake, and he even brought in the woman on horseback and she showed us where she had confronted the bow hunter. We tracked it all. But we were never allowed the time it would take to bring the various trails together. It was assumed that some local had brought in a couple bow hunters, dropped them off and picked them up again when the hunt turned sour. The big stretch was in assuming the bow hunters had been armed with a rifle."

For Detective Ringsage the clues were finally adding up to something. What he thought he had was a couple of rogue hunters who were armed with a rifle and one had committed murder. He was dead set on proving his theory.

⊕ ⊕ ⊕

Craig Ward, issuing a press release to the media under the letterhead of the Wheeler County Sheriff's Office, strongly urged the party or parties responsible for killing Phil Brooks to come forward. He quoted Tom Cutsforth as promising, "It will go much easier on them, both in terms of how the justice system deals with them as well as their own conscience. If they wait for us to catch them, it will be too late."

Deputy Ward went on, quoting himself as saying the suspects, "left a much better trail than they know."

⊕ ⊕ ⊕

After the autopsy the body of Phil Brooks was transferred from Portland to the Prineville Funeral Home. Four days later the funeral was held and Phil was buried at the ranch cemetery near the headquarters of the Fopiano. His headstone, depicting a cowboy on a horse, dog trotting alongside and pushing a small herd of cows and calves in front of him through the sagebrush hills of Waterman Flat, would be added later.

"Phil had mentioned to Wendy he wanted to be buried with what Grandpa Parton had given him, and for the longest time we couldn't think what that could be," said Tina. "And then we were going through a briefcase where Phil kept his 'important papers' and we found a knife. Grandpa Parton had given Phil that knife, and rather than carry it with him and take a chance of losing it, he had kept it in his briefcase. We buried him with the knife in his pocket.

"Our family wanted to have an open casket, but the funeral director said he would advise against it because of the amount of time that had passed and the deterioration of the body. We just went along with what we were told to do—it was such an emotional time for all of us—but later we regretted, as a family, that we did not insist on viewing Phil one last time."

A big crowd attended the funeral at the Fopiano Ranch and loud music was played on a pickup stereo with the doors thrown wide open. Law enforcement attended; some officers were dressed in uniform, and others, hoping to blend into the crowd, were dressed casually in boots, blue jeans, long sleeved shirts and cowboy hats. But they were too clean, their hair cut too short, and they stuck out like sore thumbs. Also in attendance were several women Phil had dated, and the police dutifully noted each who cried, and if a man had accompanied the woman, the cops watched to see if he exhibited any signs of jealousy.

The obituary was read and it was noted Phil had been born in Prineville on May 6, 1971, graduated from Mitchell High School with the class of 1989, and that he had worked for Cannon Tire Center in Mitchell, one of the first Les Schwab stores in existence. Phil also worked for Fran Cherry on the Cherry Creek Ranch where he herded sheep one winter, as a logger for Johnny Rhoden and F.M.C. Logging and Jim Smith and Smith Logging before signing on as a ranch hand on the Fopiano. His hobbies were listed as hunting, fishing and fixing up old rigs. His passion was simply, "the outdoors."

Dan Cannon, owner of Cannon Tire Center and a noted local cowboy poet, read a poem written by Shelli Brooks, Justin's wife, titled *My Other Brother*.

> *As I was growing up I had a wonderful brother.*
> *When I got married I was blessed with another.*

Phil was always coming over, many times a week.
The first thing he said when he walked through the door
*   was "Honey I'm home, when do we eat."*
He was always on his best behavior at the house, because
*   he usually wanted dinner.*
I must not have done too awful badly. I didn't notice
*   him getting thinner.*
Phil grew up to be a very large man!
And when feeling strongly about some things, he wasn't
*   afraid to make a stand.*
We all feel this is what happened.
We'll all miss him so.
We won't say good-bye and won't ever let him go.
Phil will always be with us each and every day.
So I'm ending this now with only one more thing to say.
We all have our memories and a special place where
*   they are held.*
How he touched our hearts and the way it always felt.

After the service concluded, Tom Cutsforth approached Jim Brooks and asked if the family would gather in one place, that he had something to tell them. Jim fixed him with a steely gaze and his deep voice rumbled as he said, "Mister, this ain't the time and this ain't the place. You best wait until tomorrow and call the house. Today I'm havin' to put my boy in the ground."

⊕ ⊕ ⊕

Mike Williams, who along with his wife Roetta held the hunting rights on the Fopiano, contacted Detective Ringsage and claimed he had heard rumors the investigation was focusing on an unknown bow hunter. He said he had some pertinent information to the case that he was sure would prove helpful. He identified Bob Long, a well-known bow hunter and big game moviemaker from the San Francisco area, claiming the Californian had been sneaking onto the Fopiano and that he had solid evidence to back up his claim. This information interested Detective Ringsage a great deal.

The trouble with this sudden revelation was that Jerry Brauns, a New York attorney representing two bow hunters from California, one of which was Bob Long, had already contacted Tom Cutsforth and was in the process of negotiating an agreement whereby his clients would be given immunity from prosecution on trespass charges in exchange for their testimony.

⊕ ⊕ ⊕

The day after Phil was laid to rest, Tom Cutsforth and Otho Caldera visited the Brooks family at their ranch west of Mitchell. Otho seemed uncomfortable in this setting and the district attorney did most of the talking. He said a New York attorney, representing two bow hunters from California, had contacted him and the two men had been given immunity in exchange for their testimony. He seemed very pleased with himself when he said, "They were on the Fopiano and might know something that will aid the investigation."

Tina was at the house that day and she bristled at this announcement. She pushed back. "We asked to see Phil's body. You won't let us. Then the funeral home insisted on a closed casket. We went along with that, too. We hear all the rumors about the leads you're following and the people you're talking to, and you tell us nothing. We hear the results of the autopsy on the radio. We read about things in the newspapers. We see you on television. We are Phil's family and we don't appreciate being the last to know. If you want to be a big shot and stand up in front of the TV camera and dish out information to the reporters that's fine, but call us personally, let us know what's going on rather than make us read about it, or hear about it, or see it on TV."

Tom Cutsforth hung his head and muttered, "I'm sorry. Guess I got caught up in all the publicity."

⊕ ⊕ ⊕

Bill Smith, a major Bend developer and owner of the G-I Ranch south of Paulina, heard about the missing cowboy and the fact local law enforcement and the state police had not been able to locate a viable suspect. He made a few phone calls and in a short time put together a reward fund that eventually reached $65,000, the largest reward ever offered in the state of Oregon.

"When the reward failed to generate any solid leads, we offered to increase the amount," stated Bill, "but the state police said it wouldn't do any good, so we left it where it was."

Those who contributed included the Brooks family, friends of the family, local ranchers and the owners of car dealerships, sawmills and even Nosler Bullets, Inc. of Bend. Of course, William Smith Properties, Inc. and the G-I Ranch were included on the list but the largest single contributor was Jack Rhoden, who owned the sprawling 43,000 acre Sixshooter Ranch next door to the Fopiano.

"Why was I willing to pony up twenty grand? Because I wanted to help find the killer," said Jack. "But that was before the state cops went off the deep end and announced to the world one of my sons was a suspect."

⊕ ⊕ ⊕

"The day Phil got killed was my birthday," said Jimmy Collins. "After we moved cows, Phil took the afternoon off to ride and I drove to the Scott Ranch and watched Phil's brother push dirt around with a D-6 cat. He was making a pond. Never could remember that kid's name. I called him Boots. I could remember Boots. I spent two or three hours at the dam and then I come on back home along about 5 or 5:30.

"Phil and me, we was 60 years difference in age, I was his boss, but you know, boil it down and the two of us was just good friends. Everyone liked that kid, except when he got to drinking and then according to what he told me, he got siwashed a time or two and after that he pretty much swore off whiskey. But he'd have a beer with me of a hot day. That kid, he was a hard worker, wasn't no bronc rider, not by any means, but he'd get on a wild one every now and then just to see, I suppose, if he could shake and rattle. He was the kinda kid who, if you know what I mean, liked to have a little wind blow by his ears, He could handle his horse, didn't jerk it around unnecessarily, was easy on cattle and I liked that about him.

"Told Phil he could stay at the bunkhouse—had a bathroom, hot water, electricity—but he declined and dragged that trailer of his up to the granary and camped there. Came to the bunkhouse to take showers and such. Said the reason he didn't stay in the bunkhouse was because he didn't figure my wife and I'd approve of some of the people he ran with. Don't know what he meant by that remark, might have been referring to some of the women he spent time with. But he and I never talked women, and I never saw him with a lady friend.

"One thing, I do feel a little responsibility about is this, I told Phil if he ever ran into anybody up in the hills, and that person didn't have a legitimate reason for being there, I told him to run his ass outta there. I've wondered if that wasn't what happened. If Phil didn't come across a trespasser, try to run him off and that was the one who killed him. I don't rightly know."

CHAPTER 2

The Bow Hunters

The Sunday edition of the Bend *Bulletin* carried a front-page story with a banner headline declaring that two San Francisco Bay area bow hunters, through their New York attorney, had offered to come forward to tell what they knew in the Phil Brooks homicide case. The article referred to the news release issued by Wheeler County District Attorney Tom Cutsforth as "sketchy" and went on to report that the district attorney had offered the two hunters immunity from criminal trespass charges in exchange for their testimony. The offer of immunity came with the condition the out-of-state men would forfeit any right to the reward being offered for information leading to an arrest in the Brooks case.

In the story, Tina Bolton was quoted as saying, if the bow hunters were on the Fopiano, they were obviously trespassing, and that someone had to have "planted" them there and picked them up when the hunt turned into a murder. And the district attorney alluded to preliminary evidence indicating the shooter might have mistaken the brown horse for an elk and in carefully chosen words he stated it could have been a case of "misidentification of the target." When Gary Thill, the *Bulletin* staff writer, received the news release from Wheeler County, he called to interview the district attorney but was advised, "The boss has gone elk hunting and won't be back for a few days."

In Tom Cutsforth's absence, Craig Ward was asked to comment as to whether the archers were suspects in the homicide case. He refused, offering only that, "Certain elements of the investigation began to point fingers. At that point the bow hunters came forward."

The article concluded with a statement by Tina. "I would love it if these guys can tell us who shot Phil. But we'll just have to wait and see."

Two days later, in a follow-up article, the *Bulletin* reported the two unidentified San Francisco Bay archers, "may be prepared to identify a suspect" in the murder case.

⊕ ⊕ ⊕

Gold was discovered on Eastern Oregon's Canyon Creek in 1862 and Giovanni Fopiano, an Italian immigrant, headed there with the hope of striking it rich. On the way, he passed through a high mountain valley, liked what he saw, and continued on to the gold fields, where he staked a claim and was lucky enough to unearth a rich pocket of placer gold. With his newfound wealth, Giovanni could have gone anywhere in the world but chose to double back to the high valley above the John Day River where he filed a homestead claim, built a cabin and sent for his Italian wife. Two daughters were born on the homestead, Lily and Ruby.

One day a young man came to the ranch house and asked for employment. His name, he said, was James Collins. He was an Englishman and spoke with a heavy accent. Giovanni hired the young man without knowing anything about his past. As it turned out, James Collins was actually James Raynor. He had been conscripted into the English navy, but a seafaring life did not appeal to him and when the ship docked in New York City the young sailor jumped ship and headed west. He was sure the law was looking for him, and when he passed through a Midwest town where the courthouse had recently burned, and knowing all the official records had been destroyed, James went to the cemetery, looked through the names on tombstones and selected "Collins."

James Collins impressed Lily and Ruby Fopiano with his knack for poetry and his literary bent. The young women vied for his attention. Lily won out, and although it was a scandalous thing for the headstrong woman to do, she eloped with James and they were married in California. Returning to the Fopiano Ranch, the new couple began raising horses and soon started a family. During a five-year period, Lily gave birth to four sons.

One winter, storm after storm blew in across the High Desert and the snow piled deep. A front from the Arctic moved down, settled over the land, and the horses could not get to feed. They were reduced to eating willows, finally each other's manes and tails and slowly they starved to death. Five hundred horses died that terrible winter. Come spring, James started buying cattle, and the Fopiano became a cattle ranch.

⊕ ⊕ ⊕

Bob Long made his home in the San Francisco Bay area. He owned a sporting goods store and in his spare time he hunted big game, made movies of his exploits, and participated in competitive paintball wars. He was a big man, not quite 6 foot tall and weighed 240 pounds. His only run-in with the law had occurred when he received three trespassing tickets in a single year. And although not a crime, it was said he was involved in an ugly incident when he attempted to enter several trophy heads in the archery record books, but removed them from consideration after he was accused of shooting the animals with a rifle. For the most part, Bob had managed to keep his nose clean, even though he sometimes operated on the illegal side of the fence by hunting and trespassing on private property.

Bob first heard of the hunting opportunities in Central Oregon in 1991 when he met Ralph Steed at a sportsmen's show in California. Ralph had recently purchased the hunting rights on the Fopiano Ranch and Mike and Roetta Williams were his silent partners. Bob recalled, "It was Ralph's first year and he didn't have any hunting footage or promotional shots of the elk on the ranch. I offered to help him, promising to send him six paid hunters—the going rate at that time was $3,000 per hunt—and I agreed to serve as their guide and shoot video footage of the hunts. All this was in exchange for Ralph promising me a free hunt."

That fall Bob and his six paid hunters arrived on the Fopiano. For nine days the fee hunters tried to kill an elk. During this time Bob packed a camera and recorded the hunters missing one bull after another, some from a distance of less than 30 yards. According to Bob, "Ralph pleaded with me, saying, 'We have to get a bull on the ground or we have nothing.'

"I'm a hunter. I wanted to kill something. I promised Ralph I'd get him a trophy and the next morning I went out and stuck a nice one. I returned to camp, told Ralph I had hit a big bull in the femoral artery and he was still alive and bedded down. I said it would be easy to shoot video and make it into a kill scene. I wanted Ralph to pose as the hunter and suggested he tag my elk. That way I could continue to hunt. I made it clear I expected the meat, hide and head. He was quick to agree and promised to use his tag on my elk. It was all very hush-hush between us. That kind of thing really isn't legal.

"Because he was such a big man, so heavy, Ralph couldn't get around very good. But I shot footage of him stalking my bull. I even had him take a shot. When I knew I had enough to edit into a promo video, I went in and finished off the bull, a six by six with real heavy beams. He scored 320 and was the third biggest bull I had ever killed.

"As we had agreed, Ralph tagged the bull. I took the meat, leaving the head, cape and horns with Ralph so he could have it mounted. The plan was for him to use the mount to attract customers to his booth at sportsmen's shows. The understanding was the mount would be returned to me when I finished editing his video. That was our arrangement. And Ralph invited me to come up the following year and hunt for free.

"I completed the promotional video, sent it to Ralph and he was ecstatic. Then he died: heart attack I guess. Mike Williams was the one who found the body. Anyway, Mike took over the hunting operation. I called Mike and explained my arrangement with Ralph. I said I expected him to honor it and said I'd like to have my elk mount returned to me. He stalled, for two years he stalled, and then he found out the circumstances—that I had killed the bull but Ralph tagged it—and he got all pissy and refused to even talk to me.

"I played the waiting game. Finally a friend of mine, Larry Youngs, who hunted with Mike a number of times, saw Mike at the Sacramento Sportsmen's Show and Larry recognizes my elk mount because I had shown him the kill video. He mentioned to Mike that I sure did want those horns. Mike handed them over and told Larry to give them to me.

"If you want to know where the bad blood between Mike and me started, that was probably it. Add to that, Mike found out I had sneaked onto the Fopiano and hunted. In my defense, I didn't consider I was trespassing. Ralph and I had a deal. I had a free hunt coming. Mike just wouldn't honor it, but he was still using my promotional video.

"I hunted the ranch two years, '92 and '93. The first year I got skunked. The next, I killed a decent bull. He went 307. When I was sneaking onto the ranch I made sure nobody saw me. I went out of my way not to leave any sign. The only way Mike found out was because one of my friends—I know who it was because he admitted it to me—said something to Mike.

"In 1994 I talked a buddy of mine, Robert Bradley, into elk hunting in Idaho and I suggested, just for fun, we swing by the Fopiano and see if we could get in a couple of bonus days hunting. Robert had hunted with me on the Fopiano the previous year, when I killed my 307 bull, and he was game.

How were we to know that this time there would be a dead cowboy and the place would be swarming with searchers?"

⊕ ⊕ ⊕

Two Oregon State Police officers visited the adjacent ranch, the Sixshooter, and interviewed members of the logging crew who advised the officers that because of the high fire danger, they were working "hoot-owl," usually arriving in the company crummy at about 5:30 a.m. and leaving for the return trip to Prineville about 2:30 p.m. The officers wanted to know if everyone rode in the crummy. The loggers answered that Ronny Rhoden, son of property owner Jack Rhoden, drove his own pickup and that Nord Evans, heavy equipment operator, stayed in his camper on the property, as did Dwane Thomasson, fire watch, who stayed in his trailer.

During this interview, Dwane said that on the day Phil was killed he had stayed at the logging site watching for fires until 5:30 p.m. and then he and Nord had driven to the John Day River to fish for bass. Nord confirmed this, and went on to say that during work hours he had run the excavator for two hours and dug a pond, hauled three loads of rock in the dump truck, and spread it on the switchback road going toward Mitchell. In the afternoon, because of a busted throttle on the cat, Ronny had called it quits and asked Nord if he could catch a ride in the dump truck to where his pickup was parked. Nord said, after that, he didn't see Ronny until the following morning.

Nord did offer one more bit of information, saying Ronny told him the morning after Phil was killed, at about 9:30 a.m., he was walking a boundary line on the north end of the meadow and thought he heard the report of a high-powered rifle. He asked if Nord had heard anything. Nord said from his many years of operating heavy equipment he couldn't hear a shot unless the gun was next to his ear. And then, just before the officers departed, Nord added, "One more thing, when Dwane and I were coming home, there along Parish Creek Road, probably would have been about 9 p.m., we saw two rigs traveling together. They were going pretty slow and pulled over to let us pass. The first pickup was white and some other color, a full-sized Chevy or Ford. There were three men riding in that rig. The other was a dark colored Ford Ranger with a canopy the same color. There were two fellows in that rig.

"We got on down the road and stopped. Those two rigs stopped behind us and turned out their lights. That was kinda suspicious behavior. Finally Dwane and I drove on to the Sixshooter. Thinking back, maybe we should have investigated the situation a little more."

After departing the ranch, both officers voiced their opinion that Nord seemed a bit too talkative. They wanted to check him out further. Something else they thought was interesting was that Ronny had heard a shot. It didn't mean anything. It was just an odd tidbit of information.

⊕ ⊕ ⊕

On the morning of September 20, Bob Long and Robert Bradley left the Bay area in Robert's pickup truck. The truck, loaded for an extended hunting trip, was pulling a trailer carrying a red Yahama, 250cc, Big Wheel motorcycle that belonged to Robert. Upon reaching I-5 they headed north for Oregon, stopping in Willows about noon for gas at a Shell Service Station. Robert used his credit card and was handed a receipt. Bob remembered he had forgotten his binoculars and when they reached Redding they stopped at a K-Mart store and he bought another pair. He paid with his credit card and tucked the receipt in his wallet. They turned off the freeway at Weed and took Highway 97 to Bend where they stopped again for fuel and to buy groceries.

They turned east from Bend: Robert driving and Bob sleeping, but Bob came awake when they turned onto the dirt road leading to Waterman Flat. They wanted to check things out and drove past the Fopiano headquarters, turned around at Four Corners and came back, taking Highway 26 to a county campground. Here, a little before midnight, they unhooked the motorcycle trailer. Robert drove Bob back to the Fopiano and Bob got out with both their packs and bows and started hiking in the moonlight across the open flat toward the safety of the trees in the distance.

Robert returned to camp, switched to his motorcycle and rode the 14 miles down Waterman Road to a gate where he pushed the bike under the steel cable. He met up with Bob and they concealed the bike in the trees, covering it with camouflage netting and piling brush over the top so it could not be seen. They hiked into the hills and made a dry camp about 3:30 a.m. in a draw near the road. They slept until daylight, got up and began hunting, going in different directions but arranging to meet before the evening hunt.

They were unsuccessful on their morning hunts and when they did get together Robert said he wanted to hunt near the lake, hoping to catch a bull coming to water. Bob said he had heard a bull bugling up high and figured that was where the elk would be on a hot day. He started climbing, working his way to a high bench where a woman on horseback would confront him.

⊕ ⊕ ⊕

"Let me tell you what happened when I ran into the woman on horseback," said Bob Long. "It was getting along in the afternoon and I was working my way toward an active bull. I was within maybe a hundred yards and he shut up, quit talking to me. I couldn't get him to respond to anything. I worked my way around a hill, and when I got to a little open bench I heard crashing in the brush and thought it had to be my bull. I threw out a bugle to challenge him, got ready. A few seconds passed and all of a sudden this woman on horseback was just there. That shook me up. I wheeled, ducked behind a pine tree, ran downhill, dove into a thicket of jack pine, laid in a depression and tried to cover myself up the best I could with branches, leaves and pine needles.

"And you know what? She came after me. Ran her horse right over to where I had been and she yelled at me. 'You're not supposed to be in here, you better get out. You're trespassing.' Then she turned her horse around and started out of there. I watched her go. She went over a ledge and I lost her in the trees. But I saw her once more working her way along a ridgeline.

"She spooked me, definitely spooked me and all I could come up with was that someone had found the bike, or saw where we came in, and there were people looking for us. Wanting to get away from there, I took off walking, went less than a mile and spotted a man following a fence line. I glassed him. That was when I saw his sheriff's badge and knew the law was looking for us. At that point all I wanted was to get to camp, gather my things and get the hell out of there.

"I was like a wanted man, slipping from tree to tree; made it to camp, gathered my stuff, and wrote Robert a message on a board with a broad head because I didn't have anything else to write with. It read, "Meet me at Bike." Then I got away, found a good place to hide and was planning to wait it out until dark. While I waited, I had six horseback riders pass within a 100 yards of me. I never moved and they never saw me.

"When it was good and dark I started hiking in the direction of the motorcycle. The moon came up. I popped into a clearing and in front of me, standing facing me maybe 200 yards away, was a person. I threw up my binoculars to glass him, and he was glassing me. I was caught. My heart stopped."

⊕ ⊕ ⊕

Robert Bradley and his father owned a car dealer's license in California. They bought insurance totals, rebuilt them and sold the reconstructed vehicles to individuals or other car dealers. They specialized in late model four-wheel drive pickup trucks, working on one rig at a time, selling it when it was finished and buying another. Robert admitted it was a job and that he had no illusions of ever getting rich doing it. But working for himself allowed Robert the opportunity to take time off when he wanted, and gave him enough discretionary income to afford to go hunting. Hunting was his passion. The fall of 1994, when his friend Bob Long suggested they go bow hunting in Idaho, Robert was all for it. And when Bob thought they should swing by and hunt the Fopiano for a couple days, Robert was all for that, too.

Robert was 6 foot tall and a wiry 163 pounds. He was a hiker and weight lifter and in terrific shape. He did not hunt with a rifle, was strictly a bow hunter, and he hunted for trophy animals, not with the intent of having them listed in the record books but for his own personal satisfaction. His only run-in with the law had occurred in the 1970s when he was convicted of spotlighting and lost his hunting license for several years.

His recollection of the trip to the Fopiano the fall of 1994 was a mirror image of what Bob Long remembered. Robert said they came onto the Fopiano in the dead of night and he recalled hiking past Williams' hunting camp and did not see any sign the camp was occupied at that time. According to Robert, they continued walking for another half-mile before making a dry camp. Here they slept until near daylight when they began hunting. Robert worked his way uphill to the top of Flock Mountain, the highest point around. He jumped several elk, heard them go out, had a bull talk to him once, but saw nothing. When the day began to warm and the elk were no longer active, Robert took a long nap.

"I heard the whine of chain saws and a cat operating but that was a long way from me, all the way across the big meadow. I wasn't worried," said Robert. "But then this airplane started flying over, making one pass after another. It seemed like the pilot was searching for something, or someone. I was out in the open, more exposed than I wanted to be, and I moved under a tree where I slept until the afternoon.

"I started hunting again and saw a bull but never got close enough to shoot. I was bugling, had several bulls answering, and heard Bob bugling, too. Bob and I met up. He wanted to hunt high and I wanted to go down by the lake. We walked together for a ways and then split up, agreeing to meet in camp after dark.

"I crossed over the road and a creek, then followed a well-worn elk run up a draw and onto a bench. I angled toward the lake where I found a spot that offered the opportunity to see any elk that might come drifting out of the timber. I was sitting there glassing the countryside when I spotted a coyote. He was busy catching gophers and it was fun to watch, the way the coyote stayed so still, waiting, and when the gopher popped from its hole, the coyote leaped in the air and came down on it, trapping the gopher with his front paws and killing it with his teeth. I watched for a good half-hour and then I saw the coyote jerk his head around, put his tail between his legs and run away. I figured there were only two things that could scare a coyote that way—a cougar, or a human—and glassing in the direction the coyote had looked I saw a man on horseback 300 yards away. My first thought was, 'Oh, shit!' It was not so much about me being seen—I was dressed in camo and had my face painted—but I wanted to warn Bob that someone was in there and he was probably looking for us.

"The last thing I wanted was to get caught trespassing. A country judge wasn't going to slap my hand, especially not if I'm from California. He'd throw the book at me. A trespass ticket was going to cost major bucks, and there was a good chance I'd lose my hunting license and maybe even do jail time, 30 days or something like that. I flat did not want to get caught in there.

"After the rider passed, I moved to the edge of the timber, hunkered down in a root wad, and pulled leaves, pine needles and small limbs over the top of me. I figured I'd sit tight, wait until dark, get to camp, and Bob and I would grab our gear and get gone. Twenty minutes passed, I was starting to calm down and had reasoned the rider was probably a cowboy doing his job. Then I heard noises—animals moving, brush snapping—and when I looked I saw three people on horseback coming on a line straight toward me. They had a dog with them. One rider, a woman, got within maybe 20 yards from me and stopped. She leaned in the saddle and looked right at me. The dog looked at me, too. I didn't so much as move a muscle, breathe, or blink. She rode on. The dog hesitated, and I thought it was going to come over and bark, but then it changed its mind and trotted off to catch up with the riders.

"By that time I was absolutely scared shitless. On the off chance the woman saw me and was going to double back, I decided it best to find a new hiding place. I moved a couple hundred yards and settled down to wait. I was nervous, but with dark fast approaching, I'm thinking I'm going to get myself out of this jam.

"Then right behind me, not more that a few feet away, I heard radio static and a man's voice said, 'Phil, is that you?'

"I didn't say nothing. Really, I might not have been capable of answering at that particular moment. I was too afraid to turn around and see. The voice asked again if I was Phil. This time I did turn and there was a man standing there. Now I know I'm fucked.

"He asked, 'Are you looking for Phil?', and then he must have seen my bow because he wanted to know, 'Are you hunting?'

"I said, 'Coyotes. I'm hunting coyotes.' I tried to make my answer seem believable and convincing.

"The man asked, 'Have you seen a cowboy on horseback, has a dog with him?'

"I said, 'Nope.'

"He wanted to know, 'How the heck did you get in here?'

"I said, 'Hiked in over the mountain.'

"The man said, 'Well, you best get out of here. The guy who owns this ranch doesn't like bow hunters.'

"I replied, 'Okay,' and then for some odd reason I asked, 'Who's Phil?'

"He said, 'A cowboy who got himself lost, or got hurt. Been missing since yesterday.'

"I don't know what came over me. I should have just gotten out of there while the getting was good, but I found myself offering, 'Need a hand looking for him?'

"The guy replied, 'Naw. Plenty of people are looking. He'll turn up. But you don't belong here. You best go.'

"This time I took the man's advice to heart. I walked away and found another spot to hide. I hadn't even settled in when again I heard horses moving toward me and the only thing I could think to do was climb this little scrub pine tree. I shinnied up and hung there while a dozen riders split and went around my tree. They never looked up; never saw me.

"When it was good and dark I started walking, but partway to camp the moon came up and that made me leery because it was so bright. Up in front of me, a couple hundred yards away, I saw movement and recognized it was a person. He was facing me. I looked at him through my binoculars. He was looking at me through his binoculars. It was Bob."

⊕ ⊕ ⊕

The bow hunters from California stood in the moonlight swapping stories about all the people they had encountered. Bob was still afraid they were looking for trespassers but Robert informed him they were searching for a lost cowboy. While they talked, they heard the whine of four-wheelers and vehicles on the move. The bow hunters hid as a parade of vehicles passed on the road below.

"We were going to go to camp and gather our things," recalled Robert. "But this group of people set up their camp within a hundred yards of our camp. It was just too dangerous for us to try to sneak in and get back out without being seen."

The bow hunters talked about what they had in their camp. Robert recalled, "It was all pretty much my stuff. There was some food, mostly juice, energy bars and other snacks. I had a pack frame, a sleeping bag and an air foam mattress. A couple hundred bucks worth of stuff. I didn't think there was anything incriminating and told Bob, 'Let's just leave it.'"

Bob and Robert hiked to the bike. Robert rode the 14 miles to the county campground. He drove the pickup back to get Bob and they returned to the county campground where they spent the night. Robert, who no longer had a sleeping bag, slept in his truck. In the morning they headed for Idaho, spending four days near Idaho Falls and failing to kill an elk. On the way home, in Reno, Bob called his wife, Phyllis, and she gave him an urgent message that he was to call Frank Sanders, a friend who lived near John Day, Oregon. Bob made the call and Frank didn't mince any words, asking Bob if he had been hunting on the Fopiano Ranch.

"Yeah, we slipped in there, but the place was crawling with searchers. Some cowboy got himself lost," said Bob.

"He wasn't lost," responded Frank. "He got murdered and the cops are looking for two bow hunters who were trespassing on the property."

"Holy Jesus! They're looking for us!" exclaimed Bob.

As they continued traveling, Bob and Robert talked it over. They knew they hadn't killed anyone, but the police didn't know that. And if the police found their camp, which both hunters assumed they would, or maybe they already had, was there something, anything that tied them to the case? Again they went over the items they had left behind and concluded nothing even remotely linked them to having been there, except for the note Bob had scrawled on the board, "Meet me at Bike," and of course the possibility the police could lift a fingerprint from one of the items.

Bob and Robert wanted to come forward and tell authorities what they knew, prove their innocence, but they were afraid of being arrested and charged with murder. They decided they needed an attorney. Bob, because of his association with professional paintball, had done business with Jerry Brauns, a New York attorney. When Bob got home he called Mr. Brauns, informed him of the situation and asked if the attorney could make a deal whereby he and Robert could avoid prosecution for trespassing in exchange for coming forward and clearing themselves as suspects in the murder investigation.

Mr. Brauns made a phone call to Linda Keys, the Wheeler County Justice of the Peace. She passed on his request to Tom Cutsforth. The two attorneys talked and quickly reached an agreement whereby the bow hunters would willingly come forward and cooperate in the investigation, and in return receive immunity from prosecution for trespassing. The only sticking point appeared to be the Wheeler County district attorney's insistence they not be allowed to claim any of the $65,000 reward.

"We didn't see anything. We didn't know anything. And we certainly aren't interested in claiming the reward," Bob told his attorney. "Make the deal."

⊕ ⊕ ⊕

"Detective Ringsage called Sunday evening and said Robert and I were to be at the state police office in Bend at 8 o'clock on Tuesday morning," said Bob Long. "He was very hard line and claimed we were his number one suspects. He said if we had anything to do with the murder, or if we had seen something and didn't come clean, he'd hang us. He added, because we hadn't come forward immediately, he could arrest us for hindering prosecution. He was very authoritative, very intimidating. He was an asshole."

⊕ ⊕ ⊕

"Detective Ringsage called me the same Sunday he called Bob," said Robert Bradley. "He was as nice and polite as he could be. He said he was calling to let me know we needed to bring all the hunting gear we had with us in September, especially our boots. He asked if we'd be willing to go to the ranch and show him where we hunted. I said we would, and made a point of letting him know we intended to cooperate fully. He thanked me and I ended the conversation by saying, 'See you first thing Tuesday morning.'"

⊕ ⊕ ⊕

When it appeared the bow hunters from California were not involved, Detective Ringsage began grasping at straws. He quietly contacted Laurie McQuary, a Portland psychic, and asked for her help. Laurie was the owner of Management by Intuition (MBI), a psychic consulting business. She was married to a Portland police officer and had assisted on a number of high-profile murders, missing persons and crime investigations in the Northwest. When Detective Ringsage contacted her, Laurie was straightforward and admitted she had never solved a case, but that sometimes, because of her insights, she had been able to provide law enforcement with the clues they needed to help them solve a case. And as she always did when working with law enforcement, she agreed to work on the Phil Brooks case pro bono.

"I asked Robb to provide me with a picture of Phil, his date of birth and a general sense of what had transpired at the scene of the crime," said Laurie. "When he provided me those things—that is all I really need in order to form pictures in my mind—I went to work."

Laurie put together a comprehensive profile of Phil and listed those things that were revealed to her through her extrasensory powers. She referred to these as "hits." Some of the most interesting "hits" were that she wondered about someone flying in and out to do the deed, questioned whether revenge or jealousy were involved, thought Phil had fathered a child recently or that someone had claimed he had fathered a child, and she saw a four-by-four pickup truck leaving the scene of the crime. She also stated that certain words were important. She listed those words as: "water man," "six shooter," and "bear away."

"Images and words pop into my consciousness," said Laurie. "I can't explain them or say where they come from. But in the Phil Brooks case I had definite strong 'hits' that this was something pre-planned, a 'committed' woman was implicated in some way, and that whoever did the deed was a bad dude and a 'champion' shot. Furthermore, I felt Phil knew about an illegal activity on that ranch or the adjoining ranch. I wondered if it had something to do with elk—an underground hunting ring where, for so many thousands of dollars, a hunter is guaranteed a trophy elk. I clearly saw that when Phil was in a bar and was drinking, he liked to shoot off his mouth. He could have said something to the wrong person, or the wrong person overheard him say something about what was going on, or what he suspected was going on. Did these people decided to get rid of him; that he was too big a liability and as long as he was alive he put the operation at risk? I don't know.

"I am positive Phil knew the shooter. In my opinion this was not a stranger-to-stranger thing. This was a deliberate act. I believe Phil was shot from a distance of a hundred yards and that a radio or telephone was used in the commission of the crime. There were at least two people involved, communicating, and I think two shots were fired at Phil and that a bullet is lodged in a tree, or a stump, or a fence post.

"Some people assume I research a case—read articles in the newspaper or go on the Internet—but I never do that. What comes to me, just comes to me. In the case of Phil Brooks, I prepared a list of my impressions and/or questions that I sent to Robb Ringsage, along with a request he provide me a detailed response. It took him a while to get back to me."

⊕ ⊕ ⊕

Bob and Robert arrived in Central Oregon, and since their scheduled meeting with the state police was still hours away, they stopped south of Bend near Lava Butte, threw their sleeping bags on the ground and slept for a couple hours. They drove into Bend, had breakfast and arrived at the state police headquarters on Empire Road at a quarter to eight. The last thing they exchanged before getting out of the pickup was to reiterate their promise to tell the truth. They knew if one of them told a lie, that lie would snowball and eventually be revealed. Robert recalled, "We promised each other that come hell or high water we were going to stick to the truth. And later, when the going got tough, we did just that."

The California bow hunters, dressed in the same hunting clothes they had worn when they had trespassed on the Fopiano, were directed to Detective Ringsage's office. Craig Ward was also there. The men introduced themselves and they all shook hands. Before Bob and Robert could sit down, Detective Ringsage read them their Miranda rights.

And then it was Bob's turn. He said, "Before we start, I want to say we're not too happy with what we read in the newspaper."

"What's that?" said Detective Ringsage. He leaned back in his chair and folded his hands behind his head. Sweat was already staining the armpits of his blue shirt.

"The newspaper said you were bringing us up here to identify the murderer," said Bob. "A statement like that puts our lives in jeopardy. We didn't see anyone. We don't know anything."

Detective Ringsage flashed his irritatingly smug smile and that effectively ended any further communication. The bow hunters were photographed and fingerprinted. Robert was told to sit and wait while Bob was taken to an adjoining room and instructed to take a seat at the head of a table. Craig Ward took notes and Detective Ringsage started down his list of prepared questions:

> *Account for your whereabouts and activities on September 20, 1994*
>
> *How did you know about this ranch and the hunting on it*
>
> *When did you arrive at the ranch*
>
> *Who was with you*
>
> *Where was your vehicle parked*
>
> *Information on vehicle used*
>
> *Where did you enter ranch*
>
> *Where did you go once on the ranch*
>
> *How were you attired*
>
> *What did you bring onto ranch*

Did you stash anything, if so what and why
Did you leave a note for someone where items stashed
What was the bike
Do you own any high-powered rifles
Did you have a rifle on the ranch, if so what caliber and
*   model*
Did you hear any rifle shots while on the ranch and if
*   so where did they come from and what time were*
*   they heard*
Did you kill an elk
Did you know the deceased James Phillip Brooks
What motel did you stay in

After all the questions had been answered, Detective Ringsage asked Bob Long if he would agree to submit to a polygraph. Bob said he would. And then Bob spoke up and asked, "Can you tell me your best estimate of when the cowboy was shot?"

"Between 5:30 and 6:30 p.m. on September 20th," said Detective Ringsage with conviction. He smiled.

"If that's the case," said Bob, "then I have absolute proof we're innocent."

"What do you have?" replied Detective Ringsage.

Bob fished three wrinkled receipts from his billfold. He held up the first receipt, said, "Willows, California, Shell Service Station, 11:31 a.m., September 20, 1994. We bought gas." He revealed the second receipt. "Red Bluff, California, K-Mart, 3:42 p.m., September 20, 1994. I bought a set of binoculars." He held up the third receipt. "Bend, Oregon, 9:53 p.m., September 20, 1994, Fred Meyer, we bought food."

Deputy Ringsage took the receipts and intently stared at them. He was no longer smiling.

⊕ ⊕ ⊕

It was Robert's turn to be called into the interrogation room. "Detective Ringsage started out being friendly and jovial. But being friendly was just not his nature," said Robert. "It didn't take long for his aggressiveness to take over. It became obvious he wanted to hang something on Bob. He asked if Bob had killed a bull on the Fopiano when we hunted there in 1993?"

Robert asked what that had to do with the murder investigation. Detective Ringsage leaned in close and whispered, "We're trying to find out if you're going to lie to us, or tell the truth."

"I'll tell you about anything that happened this year," countered Robert. "That's what we're here for. And I really don't appreciate you asking about something from the past, something we could be prosecuted for."

Detective Ringsage asked if Robert was trying to be a smart ass. Robert shrugged, said he didn't like the question. The detective again stated he was only looking at Robert's honesty and went on to say, "Bob already made a statement about the previous year. I'm just checking to see if you follow suit, or if you are going to withhold information from this investigation."

Robert's face reddened. He clenched and unclenched his fists concealed under the table. He made up his mind he would not play this silly little game and began to push himself away from the table. He stood and declared, "I've had enough of this bullshit."

"Sit down," directed Detective Ringsage while pulling out his notebook and starting down his list of questions. Robert did sit down and he patiently answered each question. He never wavered, never faltered. And as he had done in the previous interview, Detective Ringsage asked if Robert would agree to take a polygraph examination. Robert answered, "No problem."

Then, as Robert stood, he asked Detective Ringsage if he and Bob were still in trouble or whether the detective was now convinced they had nothing at all to do with the murder.

"When I asked that question," said Robert, "Craig Ward was sitting behind Ringsage and was shaking his head up and down, but Ringsage claimed we were still 'viable suspects.' Those were his words. And then rather than take us to lunch, or have sandwiches brought in, he said we could go to lunch, but to be back at his office in an hour.

"Bob and I drove south on Highway 97 and stopped at Izzy's Pizza. We walked in and there sat Ringsage, Ward and a couple of other officers, their plates piled high with pizza. I don't know how they got there so fast but I do know, at that point, the last person I wanted to see was Robb Ringsage. He was such a dick."

⊕ ⊕ ⊕

On the drive to the Fopiano, Detective Ringsage had Robert ride with him and directed Bob to ride with Craig Ward, in his Wheeler County Chevy Blazer. And while Bob and Craig had a friendly visit, about family and hunting and the sporting goods business, Detective Ringsage was making life miserable for Robert by lobbing barbed questions in his direction. He asked if Robert was an avid hunter.

"I hunt as often as I can," said Robert.

"What do you hunt?"

"Anything. Pigs to buffalo and turkeys to elk."

"Where do you hunt?"

"Everywhere I can."

"And some places where you're not supposed to. Your rap sheet says you were arrested three times in the same year for trespassing."

"That wasn't me," said Robert defensively. "That was Bob. I got busted for spotlighting, but that was 15 years ago. My record's been clean since then."

"I guess hunting on private property doesn't mean much to you. You hunt where you want to hunt. Is that the way you operate?

"Get off my case," responded Robert.

This sudden flash of anger forced Detective Ringsage to try to be slightly more tactful. He waited for a moment and asked, "Would you consider yourself a trophy hunter?"

"In my mind everyone's a trophy hunter," said Robert. "Let's say a buck and a doe are standing together, and you have a hair tag and can take either. Which are you going to shoot? Hell, you're going to shoot the buck. Works the same way with a bull or cow elk. You take the bull every time. That's just the way a hunter is wired."

"Will you pass up a small buck to go after a bigger one?"

"I really don't know what you're driving at here," said Robert. "But just so you know, I never cut off horns and leave the meat. That's disgusting. I eat everything I kill. Absolutely everything. Except for bear, can't stand bear, too sweet, too gamey. I give it all away."

Detective Ringsage went back to playing bad cop. "Why did you think you had a right to trespass on the Fopiano?"

"I didn't think I had a right," said Robert. "I just did it."

"And you thought you wouldn't get caught?"

"I didn't get caught. You didn't catch me."

"You were seen."

"I'll tell you this, Robb," said Robert. "If you ran onto me in the woods, you'd never catch me. Odds are in my favor. To be honest, you won't stand a chance."

Detective Ringsage bristled, "What makes you so sure?"

Robert shook his head, smirked, said nothing.

Again Detective Ringsage bore in with his questions. "Why do you think you have to poach?"

"Let me say it this way," said Robert. "I put in for nine hunts this year and didn't get drawn for a single one. That's what hunting in America has come down to, pay your money, take your chances. It's all about the luck of the draw. If I don't draw a tag, I certainly can't afford to drop ten grand on a fee elk hunt. Some people can. I can't. I'm not justifying what I did, or saying what I did was right. But I'm not an outlaw. I'm just a guy who likes to hunt. And let's face it, animals don't recognize artificial boundaries, they cross fences; they don't belong to any person just because that person happens to own title to a chunk of land. Animals go where they damn well please. If I harvest an elk, it's not like I'm hurting anyone."

The long ride to the Fopiano was ending and Detective Ringsage's demeanor became more lighthearted and friendly. He related a recent pheasant hunting experience he had enjoyed and now his laugher seemed relaxed and genuine. When they reached the headquarters, it was decided they would take the Chevy Blazer into the backcountry. Craig drove, Detective Ringsage took the passenger's seat, and he directed that Bob and Robert climb in back. As they neared the Williams' hunting camp, a pickup approached them.

Detective Ringsage barked at Bob and Robert, telling them to lie down in the back seat. He said, "Mike Williams is driving and he's threatened to kill you if he sees you in here. We don't want an ugly scene."

Bob and Robert did as they were instructed. Robert said, "We laid down, Bob on the bottom and me draped over him. Craig rolled down his window and he and Ringsage shot the breeze with Mike. It seemed so crazy, such a goddamn stupid thing. Here you have two armed police officers—a state police detective and a deputy sheriff—and you would think they would be capable of protecting a couple of ordinary citizens."

After conversing for several minutes, Mike continued on his way and the Blazer moved forward. Ringsage turned in his seat and said, "Okay, boys, you can sit up now."

They drove to within sight of Bearway Meadow. Craig stopped and they got out. Detective Ringsage requested, "Okay, show us where you walked."

Bob led the way uphill, passing the spot known as *the long shot*, still cordoned off with red ribbons. They hiked toward an elk wallow and as they drew near, a bull gave a high-pitched whistle followed by a throaty chuckle. Bob had the unique talent of being able to grunt like a bull elk, and he grunted. The bull answered. Bob pulled a diaphragm reed from his wallet, cupped his hands around his mouth and bugled. The bull immediately answered. The two law enforcement officers smiled broadly. Detective Ringsage was animated as he instructed Bob to, "Blow it again. Let's see if he'll come in. I want to get a look at him."

Bob bellowed. The bull bellowed. Bob whistled and the bull whistled right back. Bob was thinking, "Here we are, in the middle of a major homicide investigation, and these yahoos, instead of doing their job of trying to find the killer, are wanting to put the sneak on a bull. Go figure."

As the four men approached the elk wallow, the bull slipped out the back door and disappeared. Bob showed the officers the blind he had built, and where he had spent most of the day on September 21st. After that, the men returned to the road. They crossed over the gully carved by spring runoff, jumping over the dribble of water that was Fopiano Creek in the late fall, and started up the east side.

There were red ribbons everywhere, some in the trees and others stuck in the ground. Detective Ringsage asked Robert where he had walked and Robert pointed to a rocky ridge that was alive with red and orange ribbons and stated, "Right up there." When he said that, he noticed the way Craig Ward and Detective Ringsage exchanged glances. As it turned out, Robert had walked within 15 feet of Phil Brooks, but because he was just below the brow of the ridge, he never saw the body.

Robert continued walking. He said, "A hundred yards up the steep slope I started lengthening my stride. I wanted to prove my point to Ringsage, and finally he whistled at me, told me to hold up. It took him several minutes to climb to where I was, and when he got there, he was huffing and puffing like an old dog. I hadn't even broken a sweat."

Ringsage tried to muster a grin but failed. He said, "I see what you mean, I probably couldn't have caught you."

"Probably?" said Robert with disdain.

⊕ ⊕ ⊕

"Robert and I were nervous about taking the lie detector test," acknowledged Bob. "You just never know how a machine is going to react. I knew I was innocent, but I didn't have a lot of faith the machine knew I was innocent."

Lieutenant Lorin Weilacher, the state police polygraph examiner, attached various electrodes to Bob and placed a belt with sensors around his chest, cinching the belt tight enough Bob could not draw a full breath. Then the lieutenant went through the various aspects of the procedure and said he would ask 10 questions, ask them very slowly. Bob was instructed to wait patiently for the next question, not to fidget and to try and relax during the testing. The lieutenant promised the questions would be very specific. Responses were to be limited to either yes, or no.

"I'll show you how this works," the lieutenant told Bob. "I'll ask you if your legal name is Bob Long. You say yes, even though you know your legal name is Robert Long."

"I did as I was instructed," said Bob. "The needle jumped, making heavy black marks on the paper and I said, 'Wow!'"

Lieutenant Weilacher's next question was, "Are you from California?" That was easy for Bob. Yes. Then the lieutenant asked, "Did you hear any gunshots in the vicinity of Bearway Meadow on or about the 21st of September of this year?" Bob answered no. The lieutenant wanted to know if Bob had carried any firearms onto the Fopiano Ranch. Again Bob said no. The questions came with exasperating slowness—Did you know Phil Brooks? Did you kill Phil Brooks? Do you know who killed Phil Brooks? The wait between questions caused Bob's throat to constrict and become dry, he blinked constantly and felt sweat sliding over his ribs. The only question he had difficulty answering was whether or not he was telling the officers everything he knew about the case. He said yes, but his voice cracked and warbled like a teenager. He glanced in the direction of the graph but the line on the paper remained straight and steady.

⊕ ⊕ ⊕

It was well after 5 o'clock when Detective Ringsage approached the two bow hunters in the interrogation room and told them they had passed their polygraph tests. He said they were free to go, and as if he was making a major concession he announced to Bob he would not be pursuing charges on the bull he had killed on the Fopiano in 1993.

Bob made a gesture with his hand like he was wiping his brow. He asked, "So what made you finally believe us?"

"The receipts," Detective Ringsage said brusquely.

After that, Bob tried to make small talk. He thought he might help the investigation when he mentioned the logging operation on the ranch adjacent to the Fopiano and said, "Those loggers were only a mile or two away from where the cowboy was shot. Have you guys checked them out? Another thing, I was wondering if there were any problems, like a feud or something, going on between property owners?"

"Okay, that's enough. Get out of here," said Detective Ringsage, abruptly ending all further conversation. The bow hunters, now in the clear, departed. They headed south toward California.

⊕ ⊕ ⊕

The following day the Bend *Bulletin* carried a story about the interrogation of the bow hunters. Tom Cutsforth was quoted as saying evidence obtained from the bow hunters had allowed law enforcement to develop a list of three suspects. He did not elaborate on the nature of the evidence provided by the bow hunters nor would he divulge the names of the three suspects.

⊕ ⊕ ⊕

Larry Youngs lived in Brentwood, California and by trade was a roofer. He said, "I don't mind working from daylight until dark just as long as I can keep a separate kitty for side jobs that come my way. All that money goes into hunting trips. Either I go hunting, or I take one of my family members hunting with me. That's the one thing we can do together."

Larry and his wife, Judy, hunted the Fopiano with Mike and Roetta Williams in 1992. The following year Larry took his oldest son hunting, and the year after that he took his youngest boy. Each year they killed elk. The going rate the first year was $3,000. In 1994 the rate doubled, and Larry said he would pay that fee once but it was just too rich for him, that he couldn't throw away six grand on 500 pounds of meat.

"Detective Ringsage contacted me because he knew I hunted the Fopiano, and that I was friends with Bob Long and Robert Bradley," said Larry. "He questioned me on whether I felt Bob and Robert were honest hunters. I told him I didn't know any honest hunters; that most hunters start out honest but somewhere along the way they step over the line and do something that is considered illegal.

"The detective wanted to know if I thought Bob or Robert could shoot someone with a rifle. I told him no, they're bow hunters. They don't hunt with rifles. Then he asked why there was so much animosity between Bob Long and Mike Williams. I told him I thought it was because Bob had a lot of good connections. He made hunting videos and represented companies like Coleman that provided him with his hunting equipment for free. Mike resented that. He thought he should be getting a piece of the pie.

"In 1994, it was only a few weeks after the cowboy was killed, my youngest son and I hunted the Fopiano. In fact we hunted the ridge where it happened. Roetta Williams was our guide that day. She showed us the ribbons and pointed out where the body was found.

"Here's the whole story on that hunt. We started out from camp early one morning. There was Roetta, me, my son and an overweight, out-of-shape retired fireman named George. We walked uphill, never seen nothin'. When we turned around to come back, George decided he had to stop and relieve himself.

So the three of us kept hunting and George was going to catch up with us. We hadn't gone far when we heard this 'Kaboom!' We thought the old fart had fell down and shot himself. We ran back up there only to find that, while George was relieving himself, three big bull elk came wandering out in front of him. He shot at them. I think what happened was, he got a case of buck fever. We tracked those elk back toward the burn and that was when George petered out and decided he wanted to return to camp. Me and my son and Roetta kept hunting.

"We didn't go but maybe a quarter-mile when my boy got a shot at a nice bull, hit the elk in the jaw and we commenced to chasin' it. We went all the way to the backside of the ranch, following a blood trail all the way. We killed the bull on top of the ridge a couple of hundred yards above where the cowboy was killed. We saw all those ribbons. I asked what they were and that was when Roetta told us the story. I could tell Roetta really didn't want to be there. She kept looking around, nervous like. And once I heard the story I didn't like the place all that much either. It had this spooky feeling to it; seemed as though somebody you couldn't see was watching you.

"Every year I hunted the Fopiano we hunted the ridge where the cowboy was killed. That was good habitat and we jumped a lot of elk there. If the elk got pushed out on the upper side, it seemed like they tended to drift down to that ridge. We killed several nice bulls there.

"When Detective Ringsage talked to me he was mostly interested in what I could tell him about Bob. I think Mike had filled the detective's head with his suspicions about Bob. For instance, Detective Ringsage wanted to know about the buffalo Bob shot. He was referring to a ranch near me that kept seven buffalo and one big bull came up missing. Well, the body was there with an arrow in it but the head was gone. The cops tried to pin the killing on Bob, but he had killed his bull on the Proctor and Gamble Ranch out of Clear Lake and had it all documented on video. That was what got him off the hook.

"Then there was another incident the detective wanted me to talk about and that was a cock-and-bull story that made the rounds accusing Bob of sneaking into the San Diego Zoo and shooting a tiger. Nothing ever came of that one either. Stories like that come and they go. If a person has a little success there is always someone wanting to knock them down a peg or two. For the life of me, I don't know who might have told Mike Williams, but somehow he heard all the scuttlebutt there was to hear about Bob Long.

"Bob and I have done a lot of hunting over the years. Been to Africa together, to most of the Western states and to Alaska and Hawaii. Ever since I've known Bob he's strictly been a bow hunter. Me, I use both bow and rifle. But lately I've kinda given up the bow because of my shoulder. I can't draw back any more. Old age and a lot of hard work has done caught up to me.

"You know, I mentioned about honest hunters. Well I think it was in '94 that Roetta had her father in camp. He was 70 some odd years old. After my boy filled his tag, Roetta asked him to keep hunting and try to kill an elk for her dad. Luckily they caught an elk out in the open and her dad shot it from the road. That sort of thing, killing an elk for somebody else to tag, ain't exactly considered lawful and I really didn't want my boy mixed up in something like that.

"Another thing I remember about the '94 season is the state police came in with a military rig, had navy or air force markings on it, and Detective Ringsage stopped at our camp. He and Mike stood beside the campfire and the detective explained exactly what they were doing, what they were trying to prove. It had something to do with testing trajectory; trying to decide if a shot from a particular place could have killed the cowboy. I don't know what the results were."

⊕ ⊕ ⊕

Two old men sat in the glare of an Indian summer sun, on the white bench in front of the Wheeler County Trading Post.

One fellow said he still was of a mind those goddamn California bow hunters were somehow mixed up in the murder of Phil Brooks.

The other fellow said, "Well I know two of the three suspects the state police are lookin' at."

"Who are they?"

The second guy lit a cigarette and drawled, "One of them is Clyde Tankersley. You remember Clyde? Grew up here, a real little hellion. Guess he had a run-in with Phil. Cut him up pretty bad. What's interesting is, he's been living down in California right near where them bow hunters live. Moved back up here the week 'fore Phil got himself killed. Kinda suspicious.

"They say the second suspect is Jack Rhoden's boy. Don't know why they're after him, except Jack owns the Sixshooter. They go to tryin' ta hang somethin' on him, they best have all their ducks lined up in a row. The old man has enough socked away he can hire him any lawyer he wants, and let's face it, money talks, bullshit walks.

"Now as far as the third suspect, don't know who the hell that could be. No clue. But the cops, they'll get to the bottom of it. Probably has somethin' to do with drugs. They claim 90 per cent of the crimes committed in America are drug related. Phil mighta come up on a drug drop. Surprised 'em, got popped. Yep, that's probably what happened."

CHAPTER 3

List of Suspects

"I was bow hunting on the day Phil got killed. I wounded a bull and thought I'd give it time to stiffen up or die. Besides I wanted a little help packing him out," said Bobby Ordway, a heavy equipment operator and diesel mechanic from Spray. "I knew Justin Brooks and R.J. Scott were building a dam on Waterman Flat and I went there to see if I could recruit one of them to come lend a hand. Justin was busy pushing rock but R.J. said he'd help.

"We drove up Little Smith Hollow, were hiking in to where I figured my bull was holed up, and as I went to cross a ditch I heard the report of a rifle. It was just one shot and it sounded a long way off, like it came from up around Bearway Meadow. When I'm hunting I hear shots every now and then, even when it isn't rifle season, but this time it was unusual enough that, after I killed the bull and we were gutting it, I mentioned it to R.J. and he claimed he heard two shots. We never thought much about it until later, when we heard Phil had been killed, and then R.J. and I talked it over and the best we could come up with as far as the time of day we had heard the shot, or shots, was at a quarter to six. That was the exact same time as when the police figure Phil was killed. Was what we heard the report of the rifle that killed Phil? I don't know.

"But I did tell Detective Ringsage. He dismissed it. Said since we were six miles away there was no way we could have heard a shot fired on Bearway. I told him he was wrong, that up in that country sound can sometimes carry a long way. I've logged all over that country and know for a fact I've heard shots fired from Bald Mountain, which is a hell of a lot farther than Bearway. But Ringsage knew it all and absolutely refused to believe me."

⊕ ⊕ ⊕

Wendy Chancellor, Phil's stepsister, called Detective Ringsage to voice her concern that Phil might have confronted someone near Bearway Meadow. She said Phil respected his employers, Jimmy and Bob Collins, and if he caught someone trespassing on the Fopiano Ranch he would have run them off. But that was not the only reason Wendy was calling. She also wanted to tell Detective Ringsage that on the weekend before Phil was killed she had received an unusual telephone call. Clyde Tankersley had called from a pay phone and said he wanted to come over and visit. Even though she had not seen Clyde for a long time he was a friend of the family, anyway at one time Clyde had dated her sister, Tina.

During their conversation Clyde told Wendy he had been living in California for the past 10 or 12 years, somewhere around the Bay area, building houses but he had recently gone through a divorce, lost most of his money and had come home to get himself straight.

Wendy mentioned that Phil was already at the house visiting and Clyde abruptly said he wouldn't be coming over after all, said they'd get together some other time and hung up.

"I knew Clyde and Phil had been in a fight," Wendy told Detective Ringsage. "It happened at the bar at Spray. Clyde was up visiting his dad. He owns the bar, the Rimrock. Phil's side of the story was that Clyde and Terry Humphreys jumped him. That Terry grabbed him by the hair and threw him on the ground and Clyde cut him with a knife. Phil ended up in the hospital in Prineville. They put quite a few stitches in his cheek.

"And I heard Phil and Clyde had another run-in and a gun was involved, but I don't know the story on what happened. I don't know if there is anything to it, but I just thought you should be aware and maybe you would want to check out Clyde and see if he has an alibi."

⊕ ⊕ ⊕

On October 11, 1994 Mike Williams, who owned Battle Creek Outfitters with his wife Roetta and leased the hunting rights on the Collins' property, called the Oregon State Police headquarters in Bend and asked to speak with Detective Ringsage. Mike wanted to know how the investigation was going, and the two friends talked in general terms. Mike offered that he had been hearing the name Clyde Tankersley mentioned in reference to the killing of Phil Brooks, and stated that although he had never met Mr. Tankersley personally, he had been told that Tankersley and Phil had been in an argument that escalated into a knife fight. He went on to say he had heard another rumor—that Tankersley was guiding hunters illegally on the Fopiano. He claimed this information came from a Waterman Flat local, rancher Chet Hettinga.

The following day Detective Ringsage interviewed Chet Hettinga and the rancher readily admitted Mike Williams had flagged him down on the road and during their conversation, maybe from something Mike had said, he had formed an opinion that Clyde Tankersley was probably guiding illegally on the Fopiano. Chet said he didn't have any personal knowledge of that; it was just a conclusion he reached on his own. His assumption was that, since Clyde had been in California building houses and had just returned a week or two before Phil was killed, and the bow hunters were from

California, it seemed logical they probably knew each other. He said he had a gut feeling Clyde was more than likely the local contact and had ferried the bow hunters onto the ranch property. He admitted this was pure speculation on his part, and went on to say he should have kept his thoughts to himself instead of voicing them to Mike Williams. Chet said the last thing he wanted to do was to get mixed up in the murder investigation.

⊕ ⊕ ⊕

Clyde Tankersley was born in California and in 1963, when he was 5 years old, he moved with his family to the Mitchell area. They lived on the Burnt Ranch bordering the John Day River. Clyde was always small for his age, and lean, and tough. He had the reputation as a scrapper. After high school he dated Tina Bolton, Phil's stepsister, but they broke up and Clyde moved to California. He and his brother built houses, and as the real estate economy boomed, they developed residential subdivisions and commercial properties. Money flowed, and Clyde, who worked long hours and had an addictive personality, got into drugs. His drug of choice was crank.

Crank, an amphetamine derivative, was easy to get, fairly inexpensive and it provided Clyde with endless energy, stamina and self-confidence. When he was cranking, Clyde often mixed the drug with alcohol, a potentially lethal blend. He quit eating because he was never hungry and quit sleeping because he was never tired. But he soon found it took more of the drug, and more frequent usage, to keep him high. And when exhaustion and malnutrition finally did pull him down, Clyde was left in a deep cavern of uncertainty and depression. Drugs robbed Clyde of his money and his wife gave up on him and filed for divorce. Clyde moved back to Oregon. He arrived two weeks before Phil died.

The drugs and his helter-skelter lifestyle had aged Clyde prematurely. His hair was thinning and rapidly turning gray. He was gaunt, almost to the point of looking frail, and he was hard of hearing. Clyde, who typically dressed in cowboy boots and blue jeans, liked to wear a satin Chevy coat with the words "Heartbeat of America" emblazoned on the back. His problems with the law were lengthy and involved numerous fish and game violations, traffic tickets and three DUI convictions. There was no history of assault in his background.

"When I moved home, there was one person I went out of my way to avoid, and that was Phil Brooks," said Clyde. "For some reason the kid had it in for me. Don't know why. Don't make no sense. I knew him most all his life. His daddy raised him and his brother, Justin, to be tough little shits. They was just a couple of towheaded cowboy kids fresh off the ranch. I was around when they was growing up because I dated their stepsister, Tina. Her and I we went together. Fact is, we was gonna get married. I took her to Winnemucca to tie the knot, but I chickened out. When it came right down to it, I couldn't pull the trigger. After that, her and I, we went our separate ways. She got married, I headed south to California where I pretty much fucked up my life.

"The first run-in I had with Phil would have been along in the summer of '92. It was at a high school class reunion that I come up for. There aren't many kids in any one grade and so they throw it open to anyone who ever went to school in Mitchell. It's one big party.

"I'm standing at the bar, minding my own business, high on crank and full of booze, when Phil comes strolling in. He's this big, strappin' kid. Hell of a lot bigger than me. He comes up and tells me he's gonna kick my ass. Gets right in my face. I tell him, 'You're drunk, Phil, cool it.'

"He keeps after me until I finally give him a shove. He comes roaring back at me and I think we're gonna have a fight right then and there, tear the hell outta the place. But some of Phil's friends corral him and get him outside. I go back to drinkin' and havin' a good time. The night's still young and I aim to make the most of it.

"Next thing I know, everybody's yellin' he has a gun. I turn around and Phil is waving a six-shooter in the air claimin' he's gonna kill me. In my opinion that ain't none too neighborly a way to act. I expect him to start pullin' the trigger. Somebody's liable to get hurt, most likely me. But some of Phil's friends wrestle the gun away and shove him out the door.

"I heard Phil got so mad he jumped on the hood of his truck and stomped out the windshield of his own pickup. I know this is true 'cause I ran into Phil the next morning, took a look at his busted up pickup and I said, 'I'm goddamn glad I didn't run into you again last night. I'd hate to look as fucked up as your pickup.'

"Phil, he just laughed. I asked him if there was any hard feelings and he said no, that he was just bein' stupid. I thought that was the end of it.

"Maybe three months later I was over drinking at the Rimrock, my Dad's bar in Spray, and Phil came in with Bobby Helms. Right away I said to Phil, 'If we got any kinda problem between us, I don't wanna drink in the same bar as you.' Phil said he didn't have no problem, and so I set up a shot of whiskey for both them boys. They drank it down. I bought another round. We shot the shit. Times were goin' good, I thought, but when I got up to use the restroom all that changed.

"I was takin' a leak and Phil and Bobby came pushin' their way in there. Phil shoved me against the wall, was telling me how he hated my guts and how he was gonna bust me up. There wasn't much I could do; it was tight quarters and they're both big, strong workin' boys, 10 years younger than me. I eat crow. They called me a pussy, said I was chicken shit. I took it. Soon as I could, I ducked outta there.

"Right next to the bathroom door was the pool table and I grab me up a stick, took hold of the skinny end and get ready to fight. Them boys come out of the bathroom all laughs and giggles, but they damn sure sober up when they seen me. I swung the stick to let 'em know I meant business and told 'em, 'All right you sons-of-bitches. You want a piece of me, come get me.' They backed down. I got the hell away. Went outside, jumped in my rig and drove south of town to the bridge. I was pretty wound up. I just needed to chill. Then I come back and was gonna go to my Dad's place and sleep it off. That's what I had planned, but I ran into Terry Humphreys on the way. He was walking in the street and I stopped, got out and he and I were just jawboning.

"I never saw Phil until he rushed me, pushed me back onto the seat of my pickup and was waving this pocketknife, blade open, in my face. He was threatening to cut me up. He was on top. I couldn't move. I tried to bluff, telling him, 'Cowboy, you need a bigger knife.' That set him off, made him crazy. He screamed in my face he was the devil and was gonna send me straight to hell. Crazy shit like that.

"I tried to grab the knife. He cut my hand. Not a bad cut, but I could feel the blood all hot and sticky. I knew if I gave him the chance he'd do worse; that's the way I had it figured, and to get myself out of where I was, I head butted him. Come up hard and fast and got him a good one. Drove my head into the side of his face. His head was pinned up against the steering wheel; weren't nowhere for it to go.

"I knew I hurt Phil, hurt him bad. He pulled back; left me a little room to move and I got my feet under me, grabbed Phil by the hair and slung him down on the ground. And when I had him there, I stomped the hell out of him. I could have kicked him in the head but I didn't. Just stomped him to get his attention. Told him he didn't have no cause to be so mad at me. Told him he was an insane motherfucker. Don't know what all I said; was pretty wound up at the time. When I head-butted Phil it drove his teeth clear through his cheek. He was bleedin' bad and damn well sure was gonna need stitches. Figured Bobby could take care of him. I got in my rig, got the hell away from there.

"That's the way our fight come down, not like Phil told his folks and anyone else who'd listen. He said I was the one pulled the knife. Said I held him down, stuck the knife in his mouth and sliced him open. That shit ain't true. He's too big a boy for me to hold down and stick a knife in his mouth. No way."

⊕ ⊕ ⊕

On Saturday, September 17, 1994 Clyde Tankersley had called Wendy Chancellor and said he had no place to go. He asked if he could come for a visit and maybe stay for a day or two. When Wendy told him Phil was visiting, Clyde quickly changed his mind and said he'd find somewhere else to go.

Clyde spent that evening drinking in Prineville, and when the bars closed, he drove his Blazer toward Paulina, pulled off on a side road, and slept. The following morning he found a friend to stay with and was able to locate a job, working for Charlie Moore as a carpenter. Charlie told him he would put him to work starting the following Thursday. Clyde spent that night, and the following night, at his friend's house and on Tuesday morning, September 20, Clyde called his dad, said he had a job working for Charlie Moore but needed a few bucks to tide him over. His dad said to come on over to Spray, he'd loan him what he needed.

Clyde left Prineville at about 9:30 a.m., stopped to see a girl he knew in Mitchell for a couple hours, and took the highway over the top through the ghost town of Richmond, rather than the dirt road shortcut across Waterman Flat. He arrived in Spray and went directly to the Rimrock. At 1 p.m. he was drinking his first beer of the day. He had several more, and then went to his dad's house near the river where he read a Louis L'amour western for awhile before returning to the bar. He claimed he drank steadily until 10 p.m. when he returned to his dad's house near the John Day River and spent the night.

Detective Ringsage located Clyde in Prineville, where Clyde was living with a girl. Detective Ringsage knocked on the door and when Clyde answered Detective Ringsage asked him politely if he would mind coming up to the Cinnabar to have a cup of coffee and talk. Clyde asked suspiciously, "Talk about what?"

"We just need to talk," responded Detective Ringsage.

"Okay, give me fifteen minutes, I'll be there," promised Clyde.

"There's a lot of shit I done I ain't too proud of; a lot of shit the law might want to question me about," said Clyde. "But when Ringsage came knockin' on my door I sorta figured he wanted to talk about Phil Brooks. It wasn't no secret about the reward—65 grand is a lot of money—and there were plenty of people who wanted to get their hands on a chunk of that change. I knew my name was gonna come up at the head of the list 'cause of the run-ins I'd had with Phil. I had nothin' to hide. Ringsage asked me questions. I answered them. Then he wanted to know if I'd take a lie detector test. I said it didn't make no difference to me. Said I'd do it.

"I drove to Bend to take the test. After it was over they had me wait a couple of hours for the results. Guess they didn't believe what the machine told them. They wanted me to take it again. I told them, 'Boys, like I told you, I got nothin' to hide, let's dance.'

"The second time around they won't tell me my score or anything like that, but Ringsage said, 'Either you're the world's best liar, or you're 100 percent not responsible for Phil's death.'

"I told him, 'I ain't never been no good at lyin'. I passed your test 'cause I'm an innocent man.' And as far as the state cops were concerned, I was in the clear, but it wasn't that way out in public. I'd be havin' me a beer and some asshole would come up and want to know if I killed Phil Brooks. Like I'm gonna stand in a bar and confess. Sometimes I won't say shit, other times I'd be a little high and say I had every reason to kill him, but I didn't. It got under my skin, the accusations. Sure it did. I wanted to be left the hell alone. It ain't all that much fun havin' people think you killed someone.

"Like I said, I knew Phil when he was growin' up, knew how he was raised and I had those two run-ins with the kid. To me, when Phil got to drinkin', especially drinkin' whiskey, he was nothin' but a post-dumb cowboy. That was the way he acted, dumb as a fuckin' fence post. He could be aggressive, hell yes he could be aggressive. And if he had come upon

91

someone out there in the woods, trespassin' on the ranch where he worked, Phil was the type might come unglued and jump their ass. Hell, if he had a gun, he probably woulda shot first.

"I've heard all the rumors and then some. If I was asked my opinion, I'd say they might wanna have a long look at the money family, the Rhodens. They own a lot of ground up around there. Sixshooter ain't small potatoes. But with all that land, it don't make no sense them huntin' on the other side of the fence. And if they did cross over and got caught, what the hell difference it gonna make? Jimmy Collins ain't gonna do nothin' 'bout it.

"Some people point their finger at David Price. He's a wild card for sure. Has the same addictive problem as me—white powder—lives in a trailer there in Spray. Married to Susie, used to be Metlock. She was Phil's girlfriend back in high school. They was hot and heavy but David is the one who married her. Hard feelings? I don't know nothin' 'bout that. Maybe.

"One time here recently I ran into Jim Brooks. Told him I was sorry about all the rumors with my name attached. Said, 'Jim, I want you to know, ain't none of it true. It wasn't me.'

"Jim said, 'I know it wasn't. I think I know who killed my boy. The law they aren't doing anything about it. Who knows, I might just have to take the law into my own hands.'"

⊕ ⊕ ⊕

A story in the *Central Oregonian*, the Prineville newspaper, noted the Brooks murder was the first homicide to occur in Wheeler County in the past half century. Tom Cutsforth was quoted as saying, "One person, who is no longer a 'serious suspect' in the case came forward asking that the Mitchell, Spray and Prineville communities stop spreading rumors." The district attorney went on to confirm that Clyde Tankersley had recently passed a battery of polygraph tests.

In the article Clyde Tankersley stated, "This a very emotional situation for everyone. Let's not make any of this worse for the Brooks family, or mine. Sure, everyone knows Phil and I had some problems, but the rumors have to stop. I didn't kill Phil Brooks."

⊕ ⊕ ⊕

"I'm probably the last person, except for the actual killer, to have seen Phil Brooks alive," bragged David Price. "I was coming up Waterman Road, looked over and seen this cowboy riding a reddish colored horse, a young horse, anyway it wasn't very big, and there was a dog running along with him. I knew it was Phil; could just tell by the way he sat his saddle. He always did ride straight, yet loose. He looked like he belonged on a horse. That day he was too far away for me to holler or wave, and I didn't think much about seeing him out there, not until he came up dead."

David Price and Phil Brooks grew up together. David claimed they were like brothers. They went through school together, worked and lived together on Cherry Creek Ranch and survived a serious wreck when, after drinking for seven days straight, David rolled a pickup on the Painted Hills Road. But their relationship became strained when David married Phil's former girlfriend.

"I broke up with Phil the day after the wreck," said Susie Metlock Price. She told about the wreck, how Phil received only minor injuries and had taken a tractor from a farmer's field and drove to make an emergency call. David had gone through the windshield, had a bad cut on his scalp, broke a vertebra in his neck and had nearly severed his right hand. But Dennis Trentholm, a passenger, had been the most seriously injured. He had an ear torn off, a punctured lung and a broken back. He was flown by Air-Life to Bend.

"I kept trying to call Phil, but he never answered, and never returned my calls," said Susie. "He could be a real jerk like that, ignore me for weeks on end, and I just had enough. I gave up; never went out with him again after that. David and I started going together and we got married in 1991."

Even though Phil was invited to David and Susie's wedding, and did attend, there was always a certain underlying current of friction, and that tension erupted into a fistfight between the friends who had been as close as brothers.

"It was the same year Phil got killed. We were having a party at the gravel pit out of Mitchell. A couple dozen of us standing around a bonfire, drinking beer and having ourselves a good time," recalled David. "Phil was there. He could get a little rowdy when he was drinking, and he was drinking that night. Right there in front of God and country Phil whipped it out and pissed on the fire. I nodded toward Susie, told Phil, 'Hey, man, that ain't cool. She don't wanna see that thing.'

Phil's response was, "It ain't nothin' she ain't already seen."

"That don't mean I wanna see it again," retorted Susie.

"But then again, maybe you do," laughed Phil and he wagged his dick in her direction.

David jumped in front of Phil to defend Susie's honor. Fists flew. David recalled, "I got in a few good licks but I definitely got the worst of it. Phil beat me up pretty bad. I know I never should have yelled what I did at Phil—there were at least a dozen witnesses—that I was gonna kill him. If I'd had a gun, I might have put a bullet in him that night, but hell, in my defense, I was mad and I was beat up.

"People don't forget when you say you're gonna kill someone, especially not after that person gets killed. Every one of them people at the gravel pit probably thought I killed him. But I didn't. I don't have the balls to do something like that, kill someone."

Alcohol and drugs have wreaked havoc with David. He has been arrested for assault, DUI and convicted for a host of drug related crimes. His family has struggled to make ends meet. One time David told Susie, "You ought to turn me in for killing Phil. I'll confess. That way you collect the reward money, and you can take care of our kids and live your life. They'll keep me locked up and I can finally kick my habit."

The state police never interviewed David or Susie Price.

⊕ ⊕ ⊕

"I knew my brother," said Justin, "and if he ran into somebody up there in the woods, he'd have told them to get the goddamn hell outta there. Phillip had been in a few fights, had lost a couple and got his ass whipped. He knew better than to go to a gunfight packing a pocketknife. If some son-of-a-bitch took a pot shot at Phil, he'd hightail it outta there. If he had a gun himself, it's hard to say what he would have done, but he'd been through enough shit in his life he wasn't stupid in that way. I don't think he got shot at. I think he jumped someone and they circled around and got the drop on him. That's what I think happened. It really chaps my ass the state police didn't let the trackers finish their job. In my opinion, the cops thought they had turned up some possible evidence across the road on the hill and got all excited about a long shot. They missed the boat by not letting the Indians backtrack Phil on the ridge. Now we'll probably never know what really happened."

⊕ ⊕ ⊕

Hugh Reed was well known in Central Oregon for two unusual things, as being a former Hollywood stuntman, and for his bizarre habit of wrestling a bear in a wire cage in downtown Mitchell. He started the daily routine when the bear was just a cub. As the bear grew, Hugh never backed off, kept wrestling the bear. Sometimes Hugh won, sometimes the bear won. Once, when Phil was in first or second grade, his dad took him to the store and Hugh was there.

"Hugh is one huge man," said Jim Brooks. "He stands 6 foot 6 or so, and his arms are as big as my legs. He grabbed hold of Phil, put him in a headlock. Phil, he don't much cotton to that and he squirms, kicks his legs and swings his arms; finally works his-self free. He takes a step back, squares himself around and tells Hugh, 'Mister don't you never do that again, or I'll have to whip you.'

"Phil he was plumb serious. Hugh got the biggest kick out of that. But Phil and Hugh they was cut from the same bolt of cloth. It was not in their nature to ever back down from nothin'. Even if Phil knew he was gonna get his ass whipped, he wouldn't back down."

⊕ ⊕ ⊕

Mike Williams, as a *concerned citizen,* made yet another call to the state police, telling Detective Ringsage he might want to investigate Eric Ovens, a Prineville hunting guide who, Mike claimed, regularly hunted the Sixshooter. He further stated Eric had recently guided for the Oregon Department of Fish and Wildlife sponsored Bald Mountain Bull Elk Hunt that was purchased at auction by a Californian hunter. Mike emphasized the state police should take a real hard look at Eric as a possible suspect because he "fit the profile" of someone who might have committed the crime.

Almost immediately after this conversation between Mike Williams and Detective Ringsage the rumor started circulating that Eric Ovens was a suspect. And when Eric heard his name mentioned, he called the state police and told Detective Ringsage, "I hear you're looking for me."

"Who are you?" Detective Ringsage wanted to know.

"Eric Ovens."

There was a long pause and then the detective acknowledged Eric's name had recently surfaced as a person of interest in the Phil Brooks homicide investigation. He quickly arranged to meet Eric in Prineville. Eric took his attorney, Gary Bodie, to the meeting with him.

"Ringsage was a pushy bastard," said Eric. "He wanted to know how often I hunted the Sixshooter and I was polite and told him I'd been on that property exactly one time in my life, explaining that had been September 5th and 6th to guide the fellow who bought the Bald Mountain Bull Elk Hunt tag."

"Did you go back in there after the 6th?" Detective Ringsage wanted to know.

Eric was adamant, "Hell no, I just told you I had been on that property exactly one time and I told you when I was there. I didn't go sneaking back in there for Christ sakes."

"Tell me about elk hunting," requested Detective Ringsage.

Eric leaned back in his chair and folded his hands behind his head, elbows out. He drawled, "What do you want to know, and how much time have you got?"

"Don't be a smart ass," snapped Detective Ringsage.

This comment brought Gary Bodie to attention. He directed, "Ask your question and don't be combative or we're out of here."

Detective Ringsage flashed a tight-lipped grin. "Elk hunting is big business. What does a hunter have to pay to get an elk?"

"Depends," said Eric. "Some property owners charge by the hunter, some by the points. To hunt for the biggest trophy always costs more. Let's say you want a 350-class bull, you'll pay ten grand, maybe more. No guarantee. Maybe the bull is there. Maybe he's not. Maybe you put your hunter on the money and he's a piss poor shot. Lots of factors enter in, a whole lot of ifs."

Detective Ringsage wanted to know if Eric had known Phil Brooks. Eric responded, "Yeah, I met Phil one time at a turkey shoot up to Paulina. He was just a cowboy, country kid who'd rather be on his horse out in the hills than any place else. He wasn't much of a shot. He was hell for try, but he never won a turkey."

Eric got sidetracked, telling a lengthy story about a hunt he had guided on the Bonneview Ranch near Post. He said, "My client was a well-heeled attorney who looked like he stepped out of a Cabella's catalog, had on the prettiest shit you've ever seen in your life. I had scouted the ranch, saw this huge 7 by 7 and knew where he was hanging. I put my client on him first thing opening morning. That guy was a terrible shot, couldn't have hit the broadside of a barn at 20 paces. He emptied his rifle. The bull went up and stood there on the skyline as pretty as you please with the sun behind him, backlit with red and gold—beautiful—and this guy fumbles around pulling shells out of his pocket and trying to reload. The bull disappears. So, we go around the hill to cut him off, work our way into position and the bull is coming straight at us, a couple hundred yards out, and I tell my hunter to shoot. He tries, but his gun jams. I tell him to give it to me so I can have a look. The bull gets away. What this stupid son-of-a-bitch had done to his rifle is load his chapstick instead of a shell. There is grease and shit all over the goddamn place. I try to make light of the situation so he doesn't feel so bad. I tell him at least his barrel won't have chapped lips."

Detective Ringsage had not listened to the story. He was staring straight at Eric and he leaned across the table and accused Eric of murder. "You killed Phil Brooks didn't you?"

"I beg your pardon?" said Eric. He was still smiling from the punch line of his story but the smile faded quickly.

"You snuck back onto that property and Phil caught you and you shot him. That's what happened isn't it?"

"You're full of shit," growled Eric.

"Take a polygraph. Prove you're not lying," challenged Detective Ringsage.

"He doesn't have to prove anything," said Gary Bodie leaping to his feet. "We have nothing more to say to you, Mr. Ringsage. And you are not to contact my client ever again. Is that understood?"

Detective Ringsage nodded and he was promptly escorted from the room.

"It took a while but I found out it was Mike Williams who turned me in," said Eric. "That fuckhead. He didn't know me other than a few times I've run into him on the road when we were both hunting. I was always sociable, stopped and visited. But Mike is a bullshitter from the word go. I don't have time to waste on that cocksucker.

"I really didn't have a problem talking to the police. My alibi was rock solid. I could prove where I had been when Phil got shot and it sure as hell wasn't anywhere close to Waterman Flat. Ringsage never once asked me where I was. The problem

I had with the investigation was strictly with Ringsage. He was such a pompous, pushy little prick.

"I have a friend in law enforcement and he said in his opinion Ringsage fucked this case up coming out of the chute. If he treated everyone like he treated me I can see why. Country folk don't want to be pushed around. Intimidation doesn't work. As far as I was concerned, Ringsage was a bully, but I didn't allow him to bully me and that's why my name still comes up in the case. What a crock of shit.

"And tell me this, why did Ringsage go after me, then turn around and get a hard-on for Ronny Rhoden and try to pin it on him, but he never once looked at his buddy Mike Williams, that dickwad, and he was the one who had easy access to the property, and the only one who had something to lose."

⊕ ⊕ ⊕

Detective Ringsage interviewed Steven DeClerk, the successful bidder of the 1994 Bald Mountain Bull Elk Hunt who confirmed he had hunted the Sixshooter Ranch and on the 6th of September killed a six-point bull with a .300 Weatherby Magnum. He said Johnny Rhoden, Eric Ovens and Clay Woodward had served as his guides, and that during the hunt he was the only one packing a rifle. He confirmed he paid $12,000 at auction for the hunt and went on to add it was his understanding the Sixshooter was strictly a fee hunt ranch, but that Chuck Yeager, the famed pilot and the first man to fly faster than the speed of sound, was allowed to hunt on the ranch for free because of his celebrity status.

CHAPTER 4

The Committed Woman

Phil enjoyed his cowboy lifestyle and his freedom to come and go as he pleased. But he also enjoyed female companionship. In high school he dated Susie Metlock. After that relationship ended, Phil drifted from one woman to the next, until, like a tumbleweed coming up against a barbed wire fence, he became hung up on a local gal who worked as a waitress at the Blueberry Muffin Café in Mitchell. But Phil discovered she was a recreational drug user and dumped her, telling a friend, "I don't have no use for a woman who takes drugs."

When Laurie McQuary was putting together her profile on Phil, her psychic powers led her to believe a woman was somehow involved in Phil's murder. She was not sure about the connection and asked Detective Ringsage to investigate whether Phil was involved, even peripherally, with a woman who was already committed. By committed, she said she meant a woman who was married or involved in a serious relationship with a man.

Detective Ringsage responded. "A married woman named Cheer Painter claimed she was about 90 percent certain that Phil was the father of the child she was pregnant with. She has subsequently given birth to a boy. Cheer was estranged from her husband and advised us that she and Phil had seen each other during the last year but she had not seen much of him since March of 1994. Cheer claims Phil planned to move in with her at one time but that he eventually told her they would have to quit seeing one another. She said that he did not give her a reason for the breakup. Cheer claims her husband, John Webber, knew nothing about her relationship with Phil."

Cheer Painter, who at one time raced sled dogs and is still known by some locals as *dog woman*, had her own troubles with the law. She was arrested and convicted of mistreating horses and for cattle rustling. It came out in court that Cheer had cut the brand off a calf and sewed on fresh hide in an attempt to conceal the identity of the rightful owner. Cheer attended Phil's funeral and wrote in the guest book, "Cheer Painter and Phil's unborn child." That raised some eyebrows. And later, when she visited the Brooks ranch and again claimed she was having Phil's baby, she was run off the property.

"Cheer was looking for a free ride," said Shelli Brooks.

"Phil never spent no time with her," said Justin, "Oh, he might have danced with her a time or two at some country dance. But that was about it."

Shelli disagreed, "He might have done more."

"She claims it's Phil's kid," said Justin, "Let her get a DNA test and prove it."

"The family wanted to send Cheer packing," said Shelli. "But I love kids and I felt sorry for her. If that baby really was Phil's, and I'm not saying it was, but if it was then I thought it was so sad the child would grow up and never know his daddy. I talked to Cheer and told her if she needed us to watch the baby while she was appealing the cattle rustling charge, we would do what we could. She said all she wanted from the Brooks family was financial help. That did it for me. I didn't want anything more to do with her.

"Cheer gave the kid Phil's name, and then she turned around and told her husband, they were separated at the time, that it was his kid and not Phil's. With Cheer you never know what is true and what is bullshit."

⊕ ⊕ ⊕

Four days after Phil was murdered Cheer Painter contacted the Oregon State Police and according to the police report she stated the killing, ".... might be related to a cattle rustling case of which I was convicted and Phil Brooks was involved."

⊕ ⊕ ⊕

"I've known Phil most all his life," said Cheer. "We were neighbors and he looked up to me because I'm good with animals. I was 10 or 12 years older than Phil and we were never romantic or anything like that, not until along about in '93 when Joyce called me and said they had a field full of my horses. I went down to their ranch and kicked my horses back up on Black Butte where they were supposed to be. I was headed home when Phil stopped me and invited me to have a beer. He was living in a little cabin on the backside of his folks' ranch.

"We drank and talked about old times and a lot of things. He wanted to know if I was going to stay married to John Webber or get divorced. I told him get divorced. When I asked him what kind of woman he wanted, he said a ranch-type gal who didn't mind working. We drank a few more beers and he invited me to go to bed with him, but I thought better of it. The next time we were together we did end up in bed and after that it was hit and miss. We got together when we got together, no strings or anything like that.

"When I got pregnant I wrote him a letter. He was working at the Fopiano. A couple of weeks after he got the letter he stopped to talk to me. I saw him one more time, on the Friday before he was killed. I was coming back from John Day and Phil was turning onto the highway from Waterman Road. He was pulling his one-horse trailer and we stopped on the top of

Keys Creek summit and visited a little. He said he was headed to Madras to see his sisters.

"I was seven months pregnant and getting big; Phil patted my stomach and said he had some things to figure out but he promised he would help me. That was all he said. Five days later I heard he was missing. Then the next thing I hear he's dead, been shot. My first impulse was to suspect my husband, John Webber, thinking he might have found out I was carrying Phil's child. But John was living in Sheridan, a couple hundred miles away. All his guns were at the hockshop because he was out of money. Besides, if John suspected anything he would have met Phil and tried to beat him into the ground with his own two fists, not snuck up and shot him.

"I went to Phil's funeral and everyone, at least the Brooks family, shunned me. I was an outcast. A couple days after the funeral, I was convicted of cattle rustling. What nobody knew was that Phil had agreed to be my star witness and testify in court that he had taken care of the calf and that I had not stolen it as was alleged. I contacted Detective Ringsage at the state police office and told him Phil might have been killed over this. His response was to laugh and say, 'Nobody gets killed over rustling a calf.'

"Phil's murder definitely changed the direction of my life. I served a couple of weeks in jail, paid a fine, and when my husband begged me to give him one more chance, I finally gave in and moved to Sheridan. John was living there to be close to his father who was doing time in the federal penitentiary for dealing drugs.

"If the cops had ever come to me and wanted to have a DNA test done on my son, who was born in November and is the spitting image of Phil, I probably would have done it, even though John was dead set against it. But John is touchy about most everything."

⊕ ⊕ ⊕

According to Jim Brooks, Cheer Painter didn't have a very good reputation and he said, "What might have gone on between the two of them? I don't know what went on. Phil, he could have screwed her, but it wasn't any long running romance, I can tell you that. A gal like her pulls her pants down around her ankles in front of a young buck like Phil, what the hell does she expect is gonna happen? He's gonna poke her. I think the only reason that woman wrote the letter and come to see us was to try and get money. I sure as hell don't want nothin' to do with her, or her kid neither."

⊕ ⊕ ⊕

A buckaroo passed a table in the Blueberry Muffin Café where the locals were gathered, drinking coffee. He asked, "So what's the latest from the rumor mill?"

The head gossiper finished his sip of coffee from a white glass mug, and with a sad shake of his head, prefaced with a click from bad dentures, said, "Drugs."

The buckaroo stood holding the slip of paper with a perfect thumbprint in grease and the words, "Bacon and eggs, easy." He was in no hurry to go, knew there was more to come, didn't have long to wait.

"Drug drop. Missed the mark," said the gossiper. "Phil was in the wrong place at the wrong time. Hear tell that Webber fellar from the White Powder Ranch was involved but don't know how that could be. They still got him locked up in that gentleman's club over in the Valley. Hear they play tennis every day. Easy time. Hell, I'd like to live like that."

"Didn't know you played tennis," said one of the other men at the table.

"Don't, but I could learn. Might even like it."

And as the men talked about tennis, getting off on a tangent about pretty girls in short skirts hitting fluorescent balls around on red clay courts, the buckaroo shuffled over to the cash register in his boots with heels sloughed over, paid his bill and went outside to go about his job of pushing cows around the hills.

⊕ ⊕ ⊕

The Webber family was infamous in the history of Central Oregon. In the fall of 1988, after a 10-month investigation, nearly a hundred ATF, FBI, Oregon State Police and members of local law enforcement executed a search warrant on the Webber Ranch, located off Gable Creek, a few miles southwest of Mitchell. The kingpin, John Carl Webber II—the father of Cheer Painter's husband, John Webber III—was arrested, 46.2 pounds of cocaine worth a street value of 2.1 million dollars was confiscated, as was over $20,000 in cash and 26 handguns. John Carl and his wife were convicted of drug related charges and sentenced to federal penitentiary. John Carl did his time at the minimum-security prison in Sheridan, Oregon where his son John visited him on an almost daily basis.

After Webber's arrest, small dealers throughout Central Oregon fell like bowling pins on a busy Saturday night. Within a couple months, a string of grand jury warrants were handed down and more than two dozen drug related arrests were made, effectively crippling the cocaine and methamphetamine distribution network that had been established to feed the local area and the Northwest.

There were some who believed that even though John Carl Webber was incarcerated, he was still pulling strings and that Phil Brooks had unfortunately stumbled on a drug drop. The state police questioned several residents of Mitchell and Waterman Flat, asking if they had seen a helicopter or a fixed-winged aircraft in the vicinity of Bearway Meadow on the day Phil was killed, but the cops never gave this drug theory any serious consideration.

⊕ ⊕ ⊕

Cheer Painter reported a run-in she had in the town of Alfalfa—if a wide spot on the road with a convenience store and gas pumps out front can be considered a town—to the Crook County Sheriff's Department in Prineville. She said she took the confrontation very seriously. According to Cheer, "David Price was there. I knew he had been stealing from me and I warned him to stop. He reacted by telling me, 'If you don't back off, I'll fix you just like Phil Brooks.'

"That really shook me up, caught me completely off guard, and I didn't know how to respond. I said, 'So, you're the one who killed Phil?'

"David gave me this real hard look—he has these steely blue Charlie Manson eyes that can look right through you—and said, 'You figured it out, sister. But you'll never be able to prove it.' And he turned and walked away."

⊕ ⊕ ⊕

"I heard all the bullshit about Phil interrupting a drug drop and as far as I'm concerned that's exactly what it is—bullshit," said Jim Brooks. "It made sense with the Webbers over on Gable Creek because they had a private airstrip and everything. A drug drop on the Sixshooter or the Fopiano, that don't make no sense. What I think this thing was over was the elk; someone up there hunting illegally, maybe a paid hunter was trying to take a trophy, or maybe not, could have been as simple as someone pushing elk over the fence for hunters on the Sixshooter side. Phil caught 'em red-handed, and chewed their ass up one side and down the other. I don't rightly know what happened, but damn sure something happened."

⊕ ⊕ ⊕

After the funeral Tina Bolton tried to return to her normal life, and once again began riding Flirt on play days at the Jefferson County Fairgrounds. Flirt was not the same horse as before the killing. She was no longer like a baby, demanding attention and always wanting to nuzzle and rub against Tina. Now the little filly was withdrawn and spent her time in the company of other horses.

"When I was riding, Flirt did what I wanted her to do," said Tina. "But if someone came up and asked how the investigation was going, or if the police had found a suspect, anything like that, Flirt got antsy, shuffled her feet and wanted to move away.

"I mentioned this to my farrier and he told me about a psychic who "talks" to animals. I've never been a real believer in that sort of thing, but it intrigued me enough I did a little checking around and found an article written about this woman in *Equine Magazine*, how she could speak with animals and they would tell her things. I decided to give it a shot. I called her and told her the basics of what happened to Phil and how the horse was reacting. I also mentioned Phil had a dog with him when he was killed.

"The lady wanted the name of the horse and the dog and for me to send her a map of where Phil was killed. I faxed her the map and within thirty minutes she called back. What she had to say made the hair on the nape of my neck stand on end. I felt she did have some extrasensory powers and was really *seeing* what happened to Phil.

"For starters, she said Flirt was traumatized by what had happened, would never be the same and had basically shut down. But she said Poncho was in much better shape and described Poncho to a T—saying he was very intelligent, an Australian Shepard mix, and that he was very close to Phil. I told her Poncho had worked, ate and slept with Phil, that they were together twenty-four seven. And then the psychic described where Phil was killed, saying it was in the mountains, there were trees around, and that Flirt could see something up above—she thought it might be a helicopter—but that Poncho could not see it. What Poncho was seeing was two men and a woman sneaking through the brush. One of the men leaned a rifle against a tree and aimed it uphill at Phil. Someone said, "I can kill him and no one will ever know." Two shots were fired. The shooter, a man, was 60 yards from Phil and he was in his 40s, had salt and pepper hair and beard and was wearing cowboy boots and bright red suspenders. She described this man as "grungy looking" and a "biker type." I offered there were loggers in the area but the psychic ignored my comment and went on to say the shooter was someone Phil knew, or had worked with in the past. She also saw a light colored plaid object, maybe a blanket. I said Phil had been wearing a plaid shirt. The last thing she said was to warn me these three individuals—the two men and the woman—were very evil people. Then she asked me to send her $25 in cash and destroy any record she had ever spoken to me.

"I followed her orders. And that night, and for many more nights after that, I got very little sleep as I mulled over the clues she had given me. What puzzled me the most was not the shooter or the other man, but the woman in the wings. I wanted to know who she was, and what she was doing there. Finally I called Craig Ward, and told him everything. He said he didn't put any stock in the supernatural and advised me to let it go. That's what I tried to do, forget I'd ever talked to the psychic."

⊕ ⊕ ⊕

In the weeks after the murder Justin hunkered down and worked hard. He refused to discuss what had happened, and quit going to town because he didn't want to chance running into some well-intentioned friend who would bring up the bogged-down investigation. But Shelli, with time on her hands and Justin not around much, listened to Tina and her story about the psychic. And Shelli thought maybe, if she were to work with a psychic, she could help break the case.

"I wanted answers," explained Shelli.

"You got more than you bargained for," said Justin. "You got yourself a hell of a mountain of bills, that's what you got."

Shelli began calling the psychic hotline network she saw advertised on late night television. The psychics told her things about what had happened when Phil was killed, and about the killer. Some of the information didn't make sense, but some, when interpreted by someone who wanted to believe, made perfect sense. Shelli and Tina burned up the phone lines as they tried to decipher the clues offered by the pay-by-the-minute psychics.

"I wrote down everything," said Shelli. "They told me about the people involved and described them in detail; what they looked like, what they were wearing, what they said. One psychic even claimed the killer kept the rifle, and she gave me a string of clues on where I could find it—at the edge of a meadow, back in the trees, log cabin, beneath the floorboards, used as a residence only part of the year, nearby to the scene of the murder."

When Shelli and Tina went over the clues they were convinced the rifle was located under the floorboards of the log cabin on Sixshooter Ranch. And even though it was the dead of winter and they would have to trespass on Jack Rhoden's property, they made the decision to ride there, collect the rifle and turn the evidence over to the sheriff. They thought if they were successful this would seal the case and the killer, probably one of the Rhodens, would be tried for murder. With the weapon in hand, the killer would be forced to confess. That was the way they had it figured.

On a cold, wintry day, Shelli and Tina rode horseback onto the Sixshooter Ranch. A storm moved in, the wind picked up and it began to snow; fat snowflakes slanted down and filled in the areas between trees with a blanket of white. The two women welcomed the storm, knowing an accumulation of snow would soon wipe out any evidence of their coming and going. When they reached the cabin they dismounted, went inside the unlocked door, and pried loose a floorboard. They truly believed what the psychic had said; fully expecting the rifle that killed Phil would be concealed there. It was not. They searched the barn; still no sign of a weapon. They gave up and started for home. But as they rode, the snowstorm turned into a blizzard. They became disoriented and for several hours wandered, unsure of where they were going and finally they had to give the horses their head and allow them to find home.

This psychic lunacy that Shelli and Tina shared continued for a month, until Justin picked up the mail and found a bill for more than a thousand dollars from the psychic hotline network. His anger flared, and the fallout resulted in Shelli burning her notes from the psychics, and she and Justin separated for several months before they worked it out and were able to patch up their marriage.

⊕ ⊕ ⊕

"After Shelli pulled up stakes and took the kids with her, I lived alone," said Justin. "I had time on my hands and all this shit about Phil's murder ate a hole right through me. That was kinda surprisin' since nothin' much ever gets to me.

"I left home when I was thirteen, mostly I've cowboyed; banged around and bumped around. Shelli and I got married young, maybe too young, and so when I was all alone I went to havin' bad dreams and wakin' up in a cold sweat. It was always the same dream, that somebody was comin' after me like they come after Phil.

"One night I come awake out of a dead sleep, and there was two people standin' at the foot of my bed. Saw them clear as hell. Scared the holy shit right out of me. I jumped straight up in the air. Grabbed the rifle I slept with. Flipped on the light. But there wasn't nobody. And that scared me worse than if they had been there. It was all in my mind. I made it up. I started to shake like a bear shittin' peach pits. It was terrible. Jesus! After that night, I had to sleep with the light on. Then Shelli she moved home with the kids. I didn't need the light no more."

⊕ ⊕ ⊕

Justin Brooks drew Detective Ringsage's attention as a suspect. Adding to the detective's suspicions was the fact Justin remained vague about where he had been the afternoon Phil was murdered. The truth was, after finishing up running heavy equipment at the pond, Justin helped Bobby Ordway skin his elk. As they were working, Bobby mentioned he really didn't want to tag the bull; he wanted to keep hunting and was hoping to get something bigger in the last few days of the season. He gave the elk to Justin. Justin transported it to the Scott Ranch, hung it in the walk-in cooler and early the following morning ran the meat over to his folks place outside of Mitchell. The reason Justin didn't want to share this information with Detective Ringsage, or anyone else in law enforcement, was because he was afraid he would be arrested for transporting an untagged elk.

"Ringsage came around and accused me of killing my brother. That pissed me off," said Justin. "But if you run and hide, they're gonna think you did it. So I talked to the son-of-a-bitch because, shit, I can't afford no goddamn attorney. Ringsage asked me all these stupid questions—if I liked my brother, whether we got along, did we fight—and it was bullshit because growing up we were regular kids. Then he says my alibi doesn't fit the time frame, and I know what the deal is but I don't want to tell him. I was skinnin' and haulin' that friggin' elk Bobby killed. The folks needed meat. Anyway, I finally had to fess up and tell what I was doin' but even after that Ringsage kept me twisting over the fire."

⊕ ⊕ ⊕

Tina Bolton talked to Keith Baker and said the family had never had the opportunity to view Phil after he was dead, neither in the woods where he was shot, nor after the autopsy. She asked if Keith would meet with the family and tell about finding the body and what he learned from tracking.

"I called Otho and told him I was going to visit the family," said Keith. "He must have relayed that information to the state police because Ringsage called me and said I couldn't go. I reminded him I worked for Otho and not for the state police. He got nice, said he was now looking at Justin as a suspect and that he had a few questions he wanted me to ask Justin."

Keith met Detective Ringsage in Prineville. The detective tried to give Keith a mini-recorder and wanted him to secretly tape the meeting with the Brooks family. Keith refused, and even though he was uncomfortable doing it, Keith did accept the questions from Detective Ringsage and promised to work them into the conversation with Justin. The detective also wanted Keith to check Justin's footprint and stride and that caused Keith to smile as he thought, "He doesn't believe in tracking, or put any stock in it, unless he thinks it will help verify his scenario, and then he's all for it."

Keith had dinner with the family and he told them Phil was treated with respect and apologized for not allowing them to view the body. He explained he had rules to follow. When he went to leave, Justin and Jim shook hands with him and the women hugged him.

On the way home, Keith called Detective Ringsage from a pay phone in Prineville. The detective wanted Keith to meet him immediately, so a debriefing could be conducted, but Keith was firm. He said he was tired and it was late and he promised to swing by the state police offices the following day.

At that meeting, Keith said he had worked each of Detective Ringsage's questions into the conversation at the ranch without being obvious about it. He felt Justin was grieving like the other family members, and that Justin's wife and parents had confirmed his alibi. Ringsage pressed to know Justin's answers to specific questions, and he grilled Keith on his observations about Justin's demeanor, stance and reactions. And when Keith didn't answer like he wanted him to answer, the detective became angry.

"It's obvious you don't know how to conduct a proper interrogation," snapped Detective Ringsage.

"I never said I did," countered Keith. "An interrogation wasn't the purpose of my visit. I was there to assist the family, to answer their questions and to hopefully help them bring some closure." Keith stood and walked to the door. His parting words were, "Justin didn't kill his brother. You better look for another suspect."

CHAPTER 5

The Finger of Guilt

It was Clyde McClain's first day on the job as a Crook County deputy. He was new to the area and unfamiliar with Prineville. A call came in that a big fight had erupted at a local watering hole, the Cinnabar Lounge, and all available county, city and state police were dispatched.

"When the call came down, we rolled," recalled Clyde, "One of the deputies alerted me to the dangers we were facing, saying, 'The Rhodens are involved!'

"Not being familiar with any of the troublemakers in town, the image that came to my mind was I'd be facing a bar full of rats slugging it out."

⊕ ⊕ ⊕

Mike Williams called his friend, Detective Ringsage, at his home to say he had recently visited Sixshooter Ranch, and on that occasion had observed Jack Rhoden and his son Ronny. He said, having known them for at least five years, he was familiar with their personalities and that Jack seemed his normal self, but Ronny was strangely withdrawn and appeared to be depressed.

Actually, Ronny was inside the cabin, helping cook dinner for a group of fee hunters and never set foot outside while Mike Williams was there. If Mike was as familiar with the Rhoden family as he said he was, it would have been impossible for him to mistake Ronny for his brother Johnny. They are distinctively dissimilar in appearance and demeanor. The only logical conclusion to draw was that Mike was using his meeting at the Sixshooter as justification to call Detective Ringsage, and to point the finger of guilt at Ronny Rhoden.

"Ronny is the type who demands to be the center of attention," Mike told Detective Ringsage. "He wants to be the big shot. But when I stopped to visit, Ronny didn't say more than a half-dozen words. Something's eating at him. I think he has something to hide."

Mike went on to tell about a big buck contest in which he claimed he caught Ronny trying to cheat. At the time, Mike was operating the Mountain Country Sporting Goods Store in Bend, and along with Budweiser, he sponsored a big buck contest. Mike said Ronny brought in a monster buck rack that would have easily won the new rifle being offered as the grand prize. Mark Rhoden, Ronny's nephew, was entered in the contest and Ronny claimed it was Mark's buck. But Mike became suspicious, removed the tag tied on the rack and found Ronny's name was on the tag. Mike notified Ronny the buck was ineligible for consideration since his name wasn't entered and told him to come in and pick up the horns.

During the conversation with Detective Ringsage, Mike also claimed to have heard "through the grapevine," that Ronny had an aggressive streak: had beaten several women and one time, at Club Pioneer in Prineville, had pulled a mounted elk head his first wife had killed off the wall and destroyed the mount by breaking the nose.

Armed with this new information provided by Mike Williams, the investigators began focusing their attention on Ronny Rhoden, trying to dig up evidence that he fit the profile of a psychopathic killer. By talking to Ronny's ex-wives and girlfriends, as well as bar patrons and those who might hold a grudge against the Rhoden family, or Ronny specifically, it became all too evident Ronny's behavior would never qualify him as the poster boy for the Gentleman's Club.

One tantalizing bit of information the state police uncovered was contained in the black book Nord Evans kept chronicling his daily activities. District Attorney Tom Cutsforth convened a special grand jury for evidentiary purposes and the only person subpoenaed was Nord Evans. He was directed to bring his black book with him.

Nord handed over the diary, and some members of the grand jury seemed mildly amused and titillated with the cartoon joke on September 20, 1994 depicting a line drawing of a nude couple in bed with the man operating a camera and the caption reading, "Enough rehearsing. I've just got enough energy left for one good take."

The unusual thing about that particular page was the amount of handwritten information crammed onto the ten lines, and even scrawled on the face of the cartoon. Where other days gave a simple declaration of what Nord had accomplished, and the number of hours he worked, the entries on that Tuesday went into great detail, including an entry, "I haul Ronny to his pickup, was 2:30." The time had been highlighted to make it stand out.

When questioned about this, Nord immediately responded, "Jack Rhoden told me to fill in the details of what I remembered."

Tom Cutsforth reprimanded Nord, saying it was wrong for him to have tampered with evidence.

"How the hell was I to know it was evidence?" groused Nord. "I was just doing what the boss told me to do. Jack was helping me get it down right."

The Phil Brooks homicide investigative team seized on this information as an important key to prove Jack Rhoden was up to his same old tricks, trying to manipulate the situation to protect his son. They had other evidence that Jack had done this in the past, that he had used his influence and money to buy Ronny out of trouble.

The corroborative information gathered by the state police revealed Ronny indeed did have an aggressive nature, as well as a history of assaulting others, especially women. And on more than one occasion Jack had kept Ronny from going to jail.

Near the time Phil was killed, Ronny was involved in a nasty divorce and a costly fight over custody of the couple's two children. Lari Rhoden, Ronny's estranged wife, had pulled up stakes in Prineville and moved to Arizona with the children. When Ronny called to talk to the children, Lari made clandestine tapes of their conversations. She was perfectly willing to make these recordings available to the state police.

Excerpts taken from the recordings fueled the fire that Ronny was what the state police were now referring to as a sociopath/psychopath. On one tape Ronny was heard threatening the life of the new man in Lari's life, saying he planned to "twist him like a pretzel and kill him," and that the next time he saw him he would, "shoot him right there between the eyes," and he promised, "I'll bury his body in the woods."

Debbie B., another ex-wife, testified Ronny had held a knife to her throat, and had shot at her car when she tried to leave him. She said she divorced Ronny, "in order to save my life." And when Ronny's name was mentioned as a suspect in the Phil Brooks murder, she said she was not surprised and told Detective Ringsage, "I definitely think he is capable of murder."

And when Detective Ringsage interviewed one of Ronny's former girlfriends, Faye B., she told an appalling story of how Ronny had brutalized her, and that Jack had sought to cover up the crime. According to Faye, she had lived with Ronny for several months in 1980, and during their brief relationship Ronny became increasingly more agitated and violent.

"When Ronny was drinking he did bad things," said Faye. "One time he repeatedly hit me with a spoon while I was trying to cook his dinner. Another time he picked me up and threw me out of bed. He became so violent and intimidating that, for my personal safety, I had to move out."

She described an incident on June 5, 1980, when Ronny banged on the door where she was living and demanded she let him in. He seemed contrite and apologetic. She finally opened the door. Once inside, according to Faye, Ronny flew into an uncontrollable rage. He threw her on the floor and kicked and stomped her with his cowboy boots until he abruptly stopped and gasped, "What have I done?" Then he left the house.

Faye made her way to the Prineville Hospital, where she remained for five days. When she was released, afraid to go home, she moved in with a friend. While she was there recovering, she said Jack Rhoden called and eventually convinced her to meet him. Faye said at the meeting Jack insisted it wasn't Ronny's fault, that he had learned his abusive and shameful behavior from him. Jack admitted to having beaten his wife and he seemed very remorseful of his past. Eventually he convinced Faye to drop the charges against Ronny. According to Faye, in return Jack agreed to pay all of Faye's medical expenses, send her to Hawaii and give her $5,000 cash.

⊕ ⊕ ⊕

"I never said I was a choirboy," admitted Ronny Rhoden. "Sure, I've had run-ins with the law, but like I told Ringsage, every scrape I've ever been involved in, alcohol was the contributing factor. I'm not a happy drunk. Enough said. It seems when I drink this other person comes out. Don't get me wrong; I'm not using that as an excuse. That's just fact. I've quit drinking, sometimes for a year or more, and then about the time everyone in town starts thinking I've reformed, I have to prove alcohol is bigger than me and make a total ass of myself."

⊕ ⊕ ⊕

Ronny claimed reading Nord's diary helped him remember what he had done on that fateful Tuesday when Phil was killed. His normal workday was anything but normal. He might run lines between his father's private ground and the odd pieces of BLM ground, marking trees with paint so the loggers didn't cross over and mistakenly drop government timber. He operated heavy equipment—breaking rock loose in the pit, blading roads, opening spurs to get trucks to the log decks— and if any member of the logging crew was sick or failed to show, Ronny filled in.

After looking at Nord's diary, Ronny remembered a number of things about the 20th of September: leaving his pickup, walking the cat a mile-and-a-half to the rock pit, pushing rock for Nord, the throttle on the D-6 jamming, and riding in the dump truck to retrieve his pickup. Then he drove home.

Weeks after the fact, one day when Ronny returned from Sixshooter to the Prineville offices of Rhoden Enterprises, two state policemen, driving a Jeep Cherokee borrowed from Crook County Sheriff's Department, were waiting for him. They were friendly and asked if Ronny would mind returning to Sixshooter, saying if they were on site maybe he could explain a few things they were having trouble understanding. Ronny agreed and was directed to sit in the passenger seat while one trooper drove and the other sat in back jotting down notes.

"At that point I had no goddamn idea I was a suspect," said Ronny. "They never suggested they were looking at me, never read me my rights, nothing. I thought they wanted to eliminate any cloud of suspicion that one of my crew had shot Phil. I knew my guys were innocent, and was willing to go out of my way to prove it."

The state police officers took turns firing questions at Ronny. One asked how long it took to drive from Prineville to Sixshooter. Ronny said he generally left home about 4 a.m., and at that early hour there wasn't much traffic and never any cops. He said if he was able to dodge the deer, and if he drove like a bat out of hell, after opening and closing the gates, he could be there in an hour and a half. The cop in the back seat jotted down this information.

Ronny was asked what he had done on the day Phil was murdered, and because he had examined Nord's diary, he promptly went through his day; from pushing rock at the pit to the cat breaking down and leaving Sixshooter at 2:30 p.m., radioing the crew on the way out to warn them Nord was dumping rock on the switchbacks and stopping for a soda pop at Cannon's, a service station and convenience store in Mitchell.

"It was a hot day. Bob Cannon was sitting in his easy chair, didn't want to get up and make change, and when I grabbed a soda he told me it was on the house," recalled Ronny. "That was the only time in his life he ever bought me a soda. I got back on the road and Mike Perry, the foreman of our logging crew, called on the radio to say they were stopping at Schnee's Grocery in Mitchell. I kidded him, said they should go to Cannon's and bragged Bob had bought me a soda pop.

"I know I arrived at the office around 4 p.m. because Dad was going into the hospital the following day for oral surgery. I had to have him sign a couple checks and we had some business to take care of that couldn't wait. He was going to be out of commission for four or five days. At about 5:30 p.m. I went home, changed irrigation pipe, had dinner with Sherrie and the kids and went to bed. There was nothing out of the ordinary about that day, not as far as I was concerned."

The driver glanced in the overhead mirror, and when the policeman in back had caught up with his note taking, the driver asked Ronny if anyone could verify his whereabouts on that day. Ronny thought it a tad strange they weren't taking his word for where he had been, but he told them to talk to Nord, and that the radios only worked within 8 or 10 miles of each other and they could verify that with Mike Perry or anyone on the crew to confirm he had been within range. And of course Bob Cannon and his son Dan could vouch for him, as well as Jo Powell, the office secretary.

"How did you hear about what happened to Phil Brooks?" asked the driver.

Ronny volunteered that Fran Cherry, one of the biggest landowners in the area and a family friend of the Rhodens, had called on Wednesday morning to ask if Ronny or the crew had happened to see a cowboy, or maybe a loose horse wearing a saddle, wandering around on the Sixshooter. He went on to say Phil Brooks, Collins' ranch hand, was missing. Ronny offered to send the logging crew to help search, but Fran said there were plenty of searchers.

"I called Fran that afternoon," said Ronny, "to let him know Dad's operation had gone well and suggested Fran might give him a call. I asked if Phil had shown up. Fran said not yet, that he figured the kid had gotten thrown off his horse and was laying out there with a busted leg. The logging crew was just quitting and I told Mike to drive over to the south side of Bearway, honk the horn a time or two and listen, maybe if Phil was around, they could hear him. They gave it a try, but got no answer.

"On Thursday I had paperwork to do and went to the office. About midmorning I called Fran and asked what the skinny was on Phil, if they had found him yet. He didn't know anything new, but called back within ten minutes and said Phil had been found and he was dead. A couple hours later I learned he'd been shot."

Ronny returned to the Sixshooter on Friday and was with the logging crew when two state policemen pulled up at the logging site and stepped out of their rig. Ronny asked how they had gotten onto private property and one of the officers said they had driven over a dirt barricade. Ronny laughed and expressed his surprise they hadn't hung up their four-wheel drive. He gave them the combination to the gate so they wouldn't have to chance the barricade a second time. The policemen wanted to know if anyone from the crew had seen or heard anything suspicious. They had not. They asked if anyone had noticed any mountain bike tracks. Ronny asked, "Bicycles?" And one of the cops said no, and made reference to a fat tired motorcycle like a Tote-Goat. Again, no one had seen any tracks. After 15 or 20 minutes, the state police departed.

Ronny explained all this to the officers on the drive to Sixshooter. The state policeman who was driving the Cherokee asked if they had much trouble with poachers sneaking onto the Sixshooter. Ronny responded they patrolled the ranch diligently, everyone in the country knew it and therefore they encountered very few problems. Ronny was asked if he knew Phil Brooks and Ronny said he had only met Jim and Justin, but he knew Phil on sight and mentioned he had spoken to Phil along Waterman Road, when he saw a cowboy on foot pushing cows through a fence and he had said something to the effect of, "Hey cowboy where's your horse?"

"When was that?" asked the driver.

Ronny though for a moment and responded, "The same day he was killed."

When Ronny said that, the driver turned around to exchange looks with the officer in back. Ronny noticed this and asked if there was a problem. They assured him there was no problem. But then the driver asked, "So what happened after you had this run-in with the victim?"

Ronny jerked his head around and said, "We didn't have a run-in. I was joking him and he joked back, something to the effect they didn't always have horses on the Fopiano. We both were smiling. That was it. No big deal. Certainly not a run-in."

Upon reaching the Sixshooter, the officers had Ronny show them the rock pit, and where the crew had been logging. On the way out, they crossed Bearway Meadow and went through the locked gate and onto the Fopiano. They stopped just inside, and even though daylight was fading, Ronny noticed a square of pink ribbon on the hillside just off the road. He inquired about it and was told the shooter had stood there. Ronny got out, stepped near the ribboned-off section, and wanted to know where Phil had been. An officer pointed across Fopiano Creek, to the timbered hillside, and said it was over there.

Ronny chuckled. "I doubt it. Bullets don't fly through trees. I'm not buying your theory."

After he made that remark, it seemed to Ronny, the mood of the officers dramatically changed. They were no longer talkative. They drove in silence to Waterman Road where Ronny offered to jump out and open the gate but was told to stay put. Both officers exited the vehicle and stood in the headlights, talking. Ronny felt uncomfortable sitting there alone while the officers were engaged in their private conversation and he stepped out of the rig and around to the back to take a leak. They rode to Prineville in virtual silence and the trip ended with one of the officers asking Ronny if he would be willing to submit to a polygraph.

"I don't have much faith in those things," said Ronny, "but if it'll help clear my crew I'll take one."

"Will you do it tonight?"

Ronny glanced at his watch, commented it was 9:30, that he had been up for 19 straight hours, hadn't had anything to eat and he was going home. "I'll take it in the morning," he promised.

Ronny had mentioned his work boots were at the office and the officers asked if they could come in and take a photograph of his boots. Ronny shrugged and agreed. Then they wanted to take his picture, and Ronny sat at his desk for the photograph. After that he said, "Gentlemen, it's been a long day. I'm beat. I'm going home."

Ronny no sooner walked in the door at his residence than the phone rang. The caller introduced himself as Oregon State Police Lieutenant Lorin Weilacher. He said he was the polygraph examiner and asked why Ronny wasn't in his office. Ronny explained he was tired and hungry and would take the test in the morning. The lieutenant acted indignant, said he had the polygraph equipment set up and was ready to administer the test.

Ronny's temper ignited. "Listen, I really don't give a good goddamn whether I take your stupid test or not."

Lieutenant Weilacher back-peddled, said he supposed morning would be fine and suggested a 9 a.m. meeting at the Crook County Sheriff's Office. Ronny agreed he would be there.

"I called Dad to let him know what was going on," said Ronny. "He was none too happy and advised me against taking the test. I told him I had nothing to hide. And I didn't, but then again, I had no clue I was the number one suspect."

Ronny kept his appointment, and what he remembered most of his initial meeting with Lieutenant Lorin Weilacher was the man's horrible halitosis, and the statements he made that his polygraph machine was an infallible scientific instrument, and that as the operator he was extremely well educated and eminently qualified to read and interpret the results.

"From the get-go Weilacher and I had a personality clash," said Ronny. "He didn't like me, and I didn't much like him, or his attitude of superiority. Oh, at first he was pleasant enough. We shot the shit a little about the weather and deer hunting, that sort of thing, and then he asked if I was familiar with the polygraph and I said I was. He asked if I believed the polygraph machine gave an accurate picture of a person's truthfulness. I laughed and told him, in my opinion, it was a bunch of hocus-pocus bullshit. After that he got down to business, hooked me up and started throwing questions at me that I had to answer with a yes, or a no.

"He asked if I knew the caliber of the rifle that killed Phil Brooks. Now when Mike Williams came to Sixshooter he told Dad it was definitely a 7MM that killed Phil. I had also heard it was a .270, or a .300 Mag. Even though I had heard all these calibers I wasn't positive which might have been the right one, or if any of them were, and I hesitated but responded no.

"The next question was whether I knew who killed Phil Brooks and again I was indecisive. Dan Cannon had told me he strongly suspected Clyde Tankersley, that Clyde was a druggie and an outlaw and had been involved in a couple of knock down drag outs with Phil. Clyde seemed like the most likely suspect, but I had also heard the California bow hunters might have been involved. Again I answered no."

According to Lieutenant Weilacher, Ronny failed the first polygraph test he administered and he asked Ronny if he wanted to try a second time. Ronny agreed. At the conclusion of the second test, Lieutenant Weilacher and Detective Ringsage came into the small room where Ronny was sitting behind a narrow desk. They told him he had flunked both tests, and flunked them miserably. They said they were certain Ronny was lying, and asked if he had something to say.

"Your machine's fucked up," said Ronny.

"No it's not," the lieutenant countered defensively.

"We know what happened," said Detective Ringsage. "You were chasing a big bull, you crossed over the fence, Phil caught you and you killed him."

Ronny laughed.

"What's so fucking funny," snarled Detective Ringsage.

"You are," said Ronny. "If you think that, you're an idiot."

Detective Ringsage moved forward, until he was only a few scant inches from Ronny's face. "You think I'm stupid? I'm not the one who shot someone."

"Listen here," said Ronny, shifting to put some distance between himself and the fiery detective. "I've hunted all my life. Killed my first buck when I was eight years old. I've killed an elk on the Sixshooter each of the past 12 years. Dad has better than 30,000 acres of timberland where the elk hang; Collins has maybe five. Don't you think if I want to pop an elk out of season, I'd do it on our ground, not sneak onto the neighbors and have to drag the son-of-a-bitch over a fence? One thing about elk, they travel continuously, they may drift onto the Fopiano but they'll come back onto the Sixshooter. All you have to do is wait a day or two."

"What's to keep you from trespassing?" the lieutenant asked.

"Dad taught us the golden rule—you never cross a man's fence without his permission. I don't trespass. If I ever did, my ass would get kicked up around my ears," said Ronny. "I certainly don't need the meat. I have a freezer full of elk meat and I raise cattle. I have more meat than we can eat."

Detective Ringsage sat down. "You saw a trophy bull you couldn't pass up."

"You've been in my office," said Ronny. "You saw the bull on the wall. I killed him three years ago. He went 396 Boone and Crockett and they don't come any bigger than that, anyway not in this country they don't. I could hunt for the next 50 years and chances are I'd never see one that big again. It would have to be an absolute monster to tempt me, but then again I wouldn't do it. I've never poached an elk in my life. I've got the perfect situation. Why'd I take a chance of fucking things up?"

Detective Ringsage claimed the trackers had found Ronny's boot prints on the Fopiano. Ronny shook his head and said, "Now you're making shit up."

Detective Ringsage erupted. "Phil caught you on the wrong side of the fence. He was a big guy. You're not. You got scared. You shot him. That's what happened."

"You don't know me very well," said Ronny coolly. "I've kicked the shit out of some awful big guys in my life, and I've been whipped by some pretty damn small ones. I've never backed down from a fight in my life."

Ronny went on, "Here's the deal, somewhere along the line you guys fucked up a perfectly good investigation, and now you're wanting to pin this on me. I'm not your pigeon."

"You trespassed on Collins, didn't you?" charged Detective Ringsage.

"Hell no," said Ronny. "Like I told you, I wouldn't do that, but anyway I have permission to go on the Fopiano any time I have a need to go there. But I never have, not without Jimmy or Bob knowing it beforehand."

"I doubt that," scoffed Ringsage.

"Ask Jimmy, he'll tell you," said Ronny, raising his voice. "I'm not lying."

The lieutenant and the detective were wearing suits, and they brought in a third suit, a state police sergeant. The new man sloughed off his coat, arrogantly tossing the coat over the back of a chair. He made a melodrama of rolling his sleeves up over his brawny forearms. He turned to the polygraph machine, ripped the paper free and slammed it down on the desk in front of Ronny while screaming Ronny was a lying bastard. Ronny shook his head no. The man was so close Ronny could feel the hot spittle strike his face. He waited until the big man momentarily ran out of accusations, and then, like a wild animal backed into a corner, Ronny snarled at the sergeant, "Fuck you!" He pushed himself away from the table. His jaw was clamped tight, his fists were clenched with knuckles showing white. Ronny had been in this room, under interrogation, for nearly six hours. They had hammered him, hammered him some more, and he had finally had enough. He defiantly stood in front of the big man, leaned forward assertively and told him, "I've taken all the bullshit I intend to take. Either arrest me, or I'm walking out of here and you can kiss my ass goodbye."

Ronny flung open the door and Lieutenant Weilacher mocked him, "Running away?"

"Go ahead—arrest me," challenged Ronny. "I'll get an attorney and have the greatest fucking lawsuit this state has ever seen."

⊕ ⊕ ⊕

In his official report, Lieutenant Weilacher noted Ronny Rhoden's polygraph examination was conducted on a 5-channel instrument, and that at no time had Ronny criticized the polygraph procedure, and in fact, on two occasions had complimented the examiner and said he understood the state police had an obligation to investigate all aspects of the case; anyone who may have been involved in the murder, or who might have been in the area of the murder.

He noted the relevant questions were:
1) On September 20th, 1994 did you shoot Phil Brooks?
2) Regarding Phil Brooks, did you shoot him?
3) Excluding your shotgun, did you shoot a firearm on or near Collins' property on Tuesday, September 20th?

According to Lieutenant Weilacher, Ronny exhibited deceptive responses on the first two questions, and an inconsistent response on whether he shot a firearm on or near Collins' property. He stated in his report, "It is this examiner's opinion that Ronny Rhoden was not truthful in his response to all relevant questions in this exam. During the post test interview—about 12 p.m., I was assisted by Detective Ringsage and at this time I told Ronny that the results indicated he was not truthful; Ronny appeared to be emotionally exhausted, eyes were watery and he was somber and continued to look down at the floor and reacted very little when I told him the results that he was not truthful. For the next two-and-a-half hours Ronny continued to respond to questions concerning his activities on Sept. 20 and following.

"Ronny advised that during the early morning hours of September 20 he encountered Phil Brooks and Jimmy Collins along the road near Sixshooter Ranch on the Fopiano Ranch and they were herding cattle across the road and Brooks was on foot and Ronny said he drove alongside Brooks and said something like, 'Hey cowboy, you lost your horse?' Ronny said he did not know Phil Brooks very well but said he would acknowledge him when they did cross paths.

"Ronny said he operated a cat, pushed rock for Nord Evans for most of the day until about 2:30 p.m. and at that time he experienced mechanical problems with the throttle linkage and was able to turn off the cat with assistance from Nord. Decided to quit for the day. Ronny said he left job site alone about 3 p.m. and drove into Prineville, arriving at approximately 3:30 to 4 p.m. Ronny said he may have stopped at Cannon's store for a can of pop along the way. He said he was in constant radio communication with the crew but could not remember if the crew left before or after him. When I asked if he stopped anywhere on his way out of the job site, Rhoden answered no but later he said he may have, that he often will see elk while driving and he might stop and bugle a bull or haze the elk back onto the ranch if they were straying.

"Rhoden said he had shot 60 to 65 elk, and that he is a licensed guide. Rhoden became excited when describing his hunting skills and described the adrenalin rush experienced when he pulled the trigger on a big game animal. He describes himself as a good shot and said he can hit what he is aiming at. When I asked Rhoden about bugling elk he became angry and said he's not very good at bugling and would have a hard time doing it effectively. I reminded him of his conversation with Detective Ringsage when he bragged about how good he was at bugling, and he said he was so proficient he could do it without a bugle by using only his hand. This upset Rhoden and he denied being a good bugler.

"Ronny states he doesn't believe the Brooks shooting was accidental. He stated more than once that whoever did it, did it intentionally. Ronny said that whoever did it, did it for revenge—said someone who knew him was out to get him and said there is no way a shooter can mistake a man, a dog, and a horse for an elk.

"Ronny was questioned by Detective Ringsage about past threats he had made against his ex-wife's boyfriend, threatened to shoot him between the eyes, and Ronny admitted he had made threats and that he regretted those statements because it probably cost him custody of his children. Said since that time he has stopped drinking and is seeing a psychiatrist.

"I told Rhoden it was my belief that the person who shot Brooks had to know the area well, be an excellent shot with a rifle, and have a history with some indicators of aggression and violent behavior. He was silent and nodded his head in agreement. I told Rhoden I believed that he fit the profile of a person capable of shooting someone and walking away from it. Rhoden responded passively and responded, 'I didn't shoot nobody.'

"Midway through interview Sergeant Marlin Hein entered the room and I showed him the deceptive polygraph charts. Rhoden was very quiet and he bordered on breaking down. His eyes filled with tears and his lips quivered with anxiety. Detective Ringsage said to Rhoden, if you're not involved in this how can we clear you as a suspect? Rhoden was silent for several seconds and did not answer. Later Rhoden mentioned Clyde Tankersley, Bob Long and Robert Bradley as suspects. I told Rhoden that at one time they were suspects, but all of them successfully passed polygraph examinations that were administered by me. I asked Rhoden why he failed to pass this examination and he had no explanation.

"Sometime during the interview Rhoden made a statement that he had studied psychology in college and that he knew a little bit about it. I reminded Rhoden that he had mentioned this and went on to explain some of the verbal and nonverbal indicators that truthful individuals exhibit during polygraph examinations. I asked Rhoden to explain why his demeanor and behavior were devoid of all the mentioned indicators. Rhoden was silent and then he began to get angry with my questioning. At approximately 2:30 p.m. Rhoden stated 'I've had enough of this. Either arrest me now, or I want an attorney.' The interview was terminated."

⊕ ⊕ ⊕

"Basically the polygraph examination was like a Gestapo interrogation, jackboots and all" maintained Ronny. "They raked me over the coals for six hours; screaming, yelling and getting in my face. They accused me of being a liar and a murderer. Jesus Christ, it was the worst thing I've ever gone through and there wasn't a goddamn thing I could do except sit there and take it.

"The box spit out what the box spit out. They say the examiner can make it say whatever he wants it to say. I know he did everything he could to pin it on me and then pressure me until I broke. Whether that had anything to do with the results, I can't say. All I know is, I told the truth.

"When I walked out the door Ringsage was hot on my heels, wanting to play Mister Nice Guy. Hell, I knew what he was after, my guns. I could have told him to run his sorry ass up a flagpole—I should have told him to run his sorry ass up a flagpole—but I was just glad to be out of there and said if he wanted my rifles he could follow me home. We got there, and as he was carrying rifles to his rig, a mini-tape recorder fell out of his pocket and turned itself on. What played was the screaming match during my interrogation. He damn near dropped my rifles trying to get it turned off."

Ronny stood in his driveway, brow furrowed. He said, "That's a little odd. I don't remember you asking if you could tape me. By law, you have to have my permission. Why is it okay for you to break the law? Isn't that a little like trespassing? It sure as hell seems like you crossed over to my side of the fence."

Detective Ringsage, momentarily flustered, laid the rifles in the back seat of the black-and-white. He turned toward Ronny and said, "When I administered your Miranda rights you gave your consent."

Ronny just shook his head and let it go. He told the detective he needed the rifles returned before elk season and within a week a trooper delivered the rifles. He stated the ballistics on Ronny's rifles did not match the slug found in Phil's body, but he admonished Ronny, "Don't sell any rifles. We still have an interest in them."

Later Ronny told his father what had happened and added, 'I've bought guns, and I've given guns away as gifts, but I've never sold a gun in my life."

One of the state policemen, a local game officer, told his wife the incriminating news that Ronny had flunked two polygraph tests, and he went on to say that all but proved Ronny was the one who pulled the trigger on Phil Brooks. Armed with this information, his gossiping wife got on the telephone, dropping the bombshell about Ronny to all her friends. The telephone wires sang a lively tune, and within a few hours nearly everyone in Crook County was privy to the startling rumor that the son of one of the most prominent men in Central Oregon was going to be arrested for murder.

Ronny was tried and convicted in the court of public opinion. The state police put a noose around his neck and hung him high in the middle of the town square. And if that wasn't bad enough, a pair of state policemen went to Crook County High School, told the principal they had permission from the parents, and removed Ronny's oldest son, a freshman, from class. They did the same to the younger boy, who was in junior high. Both boys were scared and thought they were in trouble. After the fact, the state police called and left a message on Ronny's answering machine at his home saying they had spoken to the boys. A letter of protest was written to the head of the Oregon State Police, but the state police answer to no one, and the Rhodens never received a reply.

⊕ ⊕ ⊕

Jo Powell was the only office employee for Rhoden Enterprises. She had a background in banking and had served as the personnel director when Jack Rhoden's Pine Products mill was operating. Jo was considered to be very intelligent and forthright, a woman with unwavering integrity.

"Normally I leave the office and go home at 4 o'clock," said Jo. "But on the afternoon of September 20, 1994 I worked late because Jack was going in the hospital the following day and I wanted to finish the payroll and have him sign the checks.

"Ronny came in shortly after 4 p.m. I heard him talking to Jack in the back office. I never went back there, but I did hear his voice. After Ronny became a suspect in the Phil Brooks homicide, I examined our telephone records to see if he might have made any long distance calls that could substantiate his presence in the office that afternoon, but no calls were made.

"The police never questioned me. Why? I don't know. I would suppose they thought, since I worked for Jack, I would lie for him. I would never do that, not for Jack, not for anybody. Or it could be, since the state police are a male dominated fraternity, the word of a woman was unimportant to them. In their eyes, and really throughout most of Central Oregon, women are not considered equal to men. I do think my testimony would have been invaluable as far as establishing that Ronny was in Prineville at the time Mr. Brooks was murdered. I think it is unfair what the state police have done to the Rhoden family, and especially that Ronny has had to live with that ugly black cloud of suspicion hanging over his head."

⊕ ⊕ ⊕

"Hell, I grew up with the Rhodens, knowed 'em all my life," said Jim Brooks. "Back when I was a kid, Ward Rhoden and his cronies used to give my brother Ray and me two bits if we'd dog the tules for 'em. When we flushed the pheasants they'd shoot over the top of our heads and we'd have to watch where the birds fell and go fetch 'em.

"The Rhodens had that big mill, Pine Products, had money in their pockets and drove nice cars back when the rest of us didn't have shit. That burned a lot of people but it never bothered me. I stuck up for Jack lots of times, and he knew it, too. Some folks say Jack is a pain in the ass, which I know he can be, but him and me we never had no problem. One time I was buckarooin' on Big Summit Prairie, Jack come by, stopped and we must have shot the shit for a couple hours. We always been friendly like that.

"Jack's kid, that youngest boy of his, heard he wasn't worth the powder it'd take to blow his ass to Kingdom come. I know this woman lives in Prineville whose daughter went out with that kid, Ronny, and accordin' to her he done somethin' unspeakable to that poor girl. He damn near bit off her nipple. Big as shit, damn near done bit off her nipple. That right there is enough for someone to kill the son-of-a-bitch over. Far as I'm concerned he's walkin' on thin ice already. Then when his name gets mentioned in the same breath with Phil, well I don't know if this kid done it, they can't seem to prove nothin', but if I was to ever catch him in the right place, I'd tie the bastard to a tree. I think I could get him to talk. I'd cut his fucking nuts out is what I'd do. I've cut a lot of animals and wouldn't be no different for a man. Hell yes I'd do it. I'd make him talk. Just over that girl, the one he damn near bit her nipple off, that'd be enough right there for me to take out his balls. If he lives he lives. If he don't, hell, no great loss.

"You know, I say that kinda shit and I know it's gonna come back to haunt me. Just the other day I was talkin' to Joe Fitzgerald and I told him I gotta quit sayin' I'm gonna shoot the son-of-a-bitch that killed my boy. Joe said yeah, you don't wanna do that, anyway you don't wanna carry through with it cause they'd lock you up in prison. But like I told Joe, said it don't make no difference to me. I got prostate cancer and ain't got that long to live. Hell, I'm gonna die and it don't matter if I'm sittin' in my livin' room in my easy chair or behind bars in a jail cell. If I take out the one killed Phil, at least I leave outta here feelin' good."

⊕ ⊕ ⊕

Jack Rhoden was convinced Ronny had nothing to do with the murder of Phil Brooks, and as he had done in the past when his youngest son ran afoul of the law, he went out of his way to prove it. He hired two private investigators, Matt Mathews and Tom McCallum, and spent a small fortune having them interview witnesses and dig up leads that were passed on to the state police.

Jack wrote to the editors of both the Bend *Bulletin* and the Prineville *Central Oregonian* and asked that the following letter be published. Both newspapers honored his request.

On September 20, 1994 young Phil Brooks was killed by someone with a high-powered rifle while he was riding horseback near Waterman Flat. Let me say that *my sympathies go out to the Brooks family. I worked for Phillip's grandfather when I was a kid and have known the Brooks family throughout my life. The killer should be found, prosecuted and punished to the full extent of the law. But time has passed and despite a $65,000 reward, the largest in Oregon's history, no arrests have been made.*

The effects of this tragedy continue to ripple across Central Oregon. I own the property adjacent to where the killing took place and early in the investigation a member of my family was named as a possible suspect. Even though there were at least 9 people who can confirm that he could not have been anywhere near the murder scene he was tried and convicted by a jury of rumor and gossip. Law enforcement and state officials have been guilty of feeding those rumors, including the intentional release of inflammatory information and unfounded suspicions. A lot of people have listened to the gossip and are convinced they know who committed this horrible murder and that this person is getting away with it.

These unsubstantiated rumors have deeply hurt myself and my family. We want the killer identified just as much as the Brooks family does. We contributed a substantial amount to the reward fund and cooperated with authorities until it became apparent they were spreading malicious lies instead of focusing on finding the guilty party.

In an effort to do what I could I hired two separate private investigators, telling each of them they had a free hand and to investigate members of my family first. Working independently they soon became convinced that no member of my family could have been in the area at the time of the killing. They have developed several very good suspects and turned this information over to the authorities. The state police have done very little to pursue these leads. In fact their sole efforts to solve this case seems to revolve around occasionally plastering Prineville with reward posters stapled to utility poles and shoved in mail boxes and newspaper boxes.

The fact is that the investigation was tainted from the start and there is not enough solid information to point the finger of guilt at any one person. But the rumors and gossip continue and my family bears the brunt of it. Each time an article appears in the newspaper someone mails that article to us with a circle and crosshairs drawn over it.

We do know Phil Brooks was gunned down and killed and the coward who committed the crime is still walking among us unpunished for his deeds. We all want justice served. But the rumors that continue to circulate, rumors fueled by those in law enforcement, do nothing but harm to the investigation, the Brooks family and to my family as well.

It is well past time that the state police interview those people who could confirm that no member of my family could have been involved in the death of Phil Brooks. But the investigators answer to no one and instead their inaction or misdirected action only feeds the rumor mill.

Many people have suffered and continue to suffer because of this terrible murder. If anyone knows anything about the case that could help to identify the killer I ask them to step forward, get in touch with me and I will pass the information on to the authorities, or contact the state police directly. Isn't it time to put a close to this, to make an arrest and get a measure of justice?

Jack Rhoden

⊕ ⊕ ⊕

The state police profile of the person responsible for killing Phil Brooks fit into the category of *sociopath/psychopath*. Ronny Rhoden was identified as suffering from this extremely rare combination of personality disorders, although it would be nearly impossible for a person to be both a sociopath and a psychopath.

A *sociopath* is typically unorganized, cannot maintain normal relationships with family, friends and co-workers, wanders from one job to the next, lives at the fringe of society and exhibits erratic, unplanned acts of extreme violence. The inability of these individuals to plan ahead, and their lack of organizational skills, causes them to leave a trail of clues when they do commit a crime. On the other hand, a *psychopath* is obsessively organized, tends to have normal relationships with family and friends, and although they lack the ability to feel human emotions they seem to be able to understand emotions in others, and they are compulsive when it comes to committing acts of violence, often planning each minute detail of their crime to ensure they remain undetected.

Ronny's behavior did not seem to fit either category. While his office desk was a mess, he was very organized in being able to run the logging crew, take care of all the necessary paperwork and help his father oversee the fee hunting and daily operation of the Sixshooter. Ronny surrounded himself with family and friends. Outside his circle, Ronny was either well liked or despised. And according to Lieutenant Weilacher, during the polygraph examination and subsequent interrogation, Ronny did display anger, as well as the lieutenant having noted, "His eyes filled with tears and his lips quivered with anxiety." Those are all normal human emotions.

It seemed that Ronny's antisocial behavior only came to the forefront when he was drinking alcohol. He was a bad drunk. He was an alcoholic. He was powerless to stop drinking once he began. And when he was drunk, he often became belligerent, aggressive and sometimes violent. He fought men. He beat women. He broke laws. But after he sobered up, he was contrite and apologetic. His father repeatedly bailed him out of trouble, and rather than own up to his responsibilities like a man, Ronny allowed his father to throw around his influence and money. He was Daddy's boy and for some unknown reason, Jack felt a strong responsibility to protect his youngest son.

⊕ ⊕ ⊕

Rumors that Ronny Rhoden was involved in the killing of Phil Brooks continued to spread through Central Oregon like a hot brush fire pushed by a strong west wind. Tina Bolton grew fearful her stepfather would carry out his promise—if the state police could not make an arrest he would take the law into his own hands and shoot the person he figured was responsible for killing his son. She called Detective Ringsage, explained the situation as well as her fears, and asked for a favor, for the detective and the polygraph examiner to meet with the Brooks family.

When the delegation from law enforcement arrived at the Brooks' ranch west of Mitchell, Joyce Brooks directed their attention to a memorial she had made to her son. On the wall by the door was a collection of school photographs of Phil— from the kid with a silly gap-tooth grin to a proud young man— twelve photos in all, stuck to the wall with thumbtacks. Detective Ringsage, Craig Ward and Lieutenant Weilacher acted appropriately sorrowful as they filed past and on into the front room where they sat uncomfortably, side-by-side on the couch.

"We'll share what information we can," promised Detective Ringsage. "But you have to understand the current in this river runs deep and we are at liberty to discuss only the first little bit on the surface. We won't mention any names and we would appreciate it if you didn't mention any names. This will be about generalities."

"Do you think this person you are looking at right now will ever be brought to trial?" asked Tina.

"Yes," said Detective Ringsage. He went on, choosing his words carefully. "We do feel this is a case that can be made, and will be made. But quite frankly, our investigation has been frustrated by the lack of evidence we have to go on."

Lieutenant Weilacher explained the precise science of a polygraph machine and went into even greater detail explaining how a psychological profile of the killer had been generated and refined until it was established that the person who killed Phil fit under the category of a sociopath/psychopath. The lieutenant said a person suffering from this personality disorder did not think like a normal, rational person; that this type of individual might give his dog a command, and if the dog didn't obey, it would be dead. He gave another example, "Let's say you had a confrontation with this person. They might smile and walk away and you assume everything is fine and there are no hard feelings, but in that person's twisted mind they are formulating a plan to get even with you. This person does not think like you and I think. They have no conscience."

A question was asked about the person who had recently flunked his lie detector test and the lieutenant related, from memory, the three relevant questions and shared that he had asked those questions to dozens of potential suspects but only one individual had not been truthful. He said he couldn't say any more, but did offer that in the post test interview this individual was ready to break, and was ever so close to confessing, but then he snapped, refused to say any more and demanded to be represented by an attorney.

"We can't get to him," stated Detective Ringsage. "But his actions are consistent with that of a sociopath/psychopath; they will do that, switch from one personality to the next at the drop of a hat."

"I don't know how it came up, or which one said it," recalled Tina, "but one of them told us Jack Rhoden had called and raised holy hell wanting to know what question his son had trouble answering. He was told, 'To tell you the truth, sir, he could not pass the question, did you kill Phil Brooks?'"

The state police asked Johnny Rhoden, Jack's oldest son, to come in for an interview. Johnny was a big man, built like a bulldogger, and even after he was told how the police had been so aggressive with his brother, he figured he could handle himself. He agreed to the interview, but as added insurance brought along his lawyer, Steve Humphreys, just in case it turned ugly.

At the meeting, Detective Ringsage was cordial and wanted to know where Johnny worked. Johnny replied he ran his own logging show, JR Logging, and that he occasionally worked with his father and brother and was a partner with them in RoJoJack Logging.

"Did you know the victim, James Phillip Brooks?" asked Detective Ringsage.

"Yeah, he worked for me a couple of years ago."

"In what capacity did he work for you?"

"Knot bumper."

"A what?"

"He bumped knots, cut limbs off logs at the landing," said Johnny, and went on to say Phil had quit. Detective Ringsage pressed for a reason. Johnny explained it was in the summertime, during fire season, and he caught Phil smoking and told him, "If you want to pay my liability insurance you can sure enough smoke. Otherwise don't smoke."

Detective Ringsage knew more than he was letting on and revealed that when he asked, "Now, when he quit, was there any kind of wage dispute?"

"Not really," said Johnny. "Well, maybe. Two weeks before he got killed he stopped me on Waterman, him and Justin were together and my wife and my boy were with me. Phil and I were just visiting and the next thing I know he said I owed him $200. I asked what for? He said back wages. I said I always pay what I owe and that I'd have my bookkeeper look into it. I was cordial to him, didn't get upset or anything.

"This was on a Saturday and I was pretty sure Phil had been drinking. When he wasn't drinking he was a good guy to be around, but I know when he was working for me he got in fights down at the bars. For a while Phil wore a gun in a holster, even when he was bumping knots. I asked him about it, why he was packing a gun to work, and he said because someone was out to get him. He never said who it was, or if he did I don't remember."

Detective Ringsage wanted to know, "How did your brother feel about Phillip?"

"I don't think he knew him that well," said Johnny.

"Was there any kind of conflict between Phil and Ronny?"

"No. I'd have known if there was. Somebody would have said something."

"It was a long time ago, but do you remember, on the 20th of September, a Tuesday, do you remember what you were doing?"

"The only reason I know exactly is I checked on it, went back through my records and saw I drove to Bend and had work done on my Suburban. I went by High Country Four-Wheel Drive, which Mike Williams' brother owns. Scott Sabo was supposed to install a lift kit for me. He ordered in the parts and everything got put together the following day."

"Do you know where Ronny was on that Tuesday?"

"Yeah, he was in the woods."

"Did you see him at all on September 20, 1994?"

"No. I never went to the office."

"What kind of firearms do you own? High powered ones."

"I just bought a .338. I've got a .300, .270, and a .22-250."

"Have you sold any rifles since September 20, 1994?"

"I sold a .300 Browning to Jack Briggs. And I traded a .30-30 along with two boxes of shells for that .22-250."

"Does Ronny ever pack a gun in that Ranger pickup he drives?"

"As far as I know the only thing he carries is a shotgun. I saw it there behind the seat one day when I went looking for something."

"To the best of your knowledge, has Ronny sold any guns since September 20?"

"I don't think Ronny has ever sold a gun. He's kept every gun he ever owned."

Detective Ringsage took a deep breath and exhaled completely. He said, "One of the questions I wanted to ask relates to the shooting of Phillip Brooks. How do you think that shooting occurred—do you have an opinion?"

"Most likely he stumbled onto something," said Johnny. "Now I have a question for you, I heard he was shot off his horse and his hat was still on his head. Is that true?"

Detective Ringsage flashed a condescending smile. "In a homicide investigation like this we try to keep some stuff, hold back information we call it, and not allow it to become public knowledge. I wish I could tell you, but I can't."

"Well," said Johnny, "I figure Phil either stumbled onto something that was going on that could really hurt somebody, that they could really get in a lot of trouble for like drugs, but more than likely it was over elk. I've heard rumors Mike Williams had bow hunters in there. If somebody had something to lose it was Mike Williams."

"Are you friends with Mr. Williams?"

"I'd say we're friendly."

"And how would Mike Williams have something to lose? He does have the hunting rights leased on that property."

"Jimmy and Bob told him no bow hunters, period. They don't like bow hunters. If he got caught in there with bow hunters, or rifle hunters during bow season, the Collins boys would jerk his lease in a heartbeat."

"Have you ever known Mike Williams to pack a rifle when he has been in there bow hunting?"

"I don't bow hunt. I wouldn't know."

"And you have heard Mr. Williams brought in bow hunters?"

"Rumors. It's not the kind of thing Mike would shoot off his mouth about. He'd want to keep that quiet. Don't get me wrong. I'm not saying Mike did anything. That was just an example. For all I know it could have been someone who buys cattle from Collins' who saw a big bull and went after it. But I will tell you this, if Dad or Ronny or I had been in there, Phil would have come up and we would have had a conversation. Sure as hell nobody would have got killed."

"Let me ask you another question," said Detective Ringsage. "Who do you think could have done this shooting?"

"Shit, I don't know. But you guys are the ones who fed all the information to the public that Ronny was mixed up in this thing. I know Jim Brooks, know him well—he was born 200 years too late and believes in frontier justice—and if Jim knew for a fact who killed his boy that person would already be dead and buried under a rock. Is that what you want, for Jim to kill Ronny?"

"Let's not jump to any conclusions here," said Detective Ringsage, trying to be conciliatory. "We don't want Jim Brooks to take the law into his own hands. We don't want anyone else to get hurt. But we have an active case here and we have to investigate it."

"Yeah, you say that," snapped Johnny, "but you're the one who advertised it in the newspaper that Ronny was a suspect and it was the state police who fed the rumor he flunked his lie detector test. You put Ronny in the crosshairs. You all but pulled the trigger. Dad had to go over and talk to Jim Brooks, tell him it wasn't true. Jim looked Dad hard in the eye and told him, 'Jack, if I knew for a fact your boy pulled the trigger, he'd already be dead.'

"Ronny is innocent and the proof is right there in front of your face. All you guys have to do is open your eyes and look. He couldn't have been involved because he left that day in front of the crew. He got to the office. Jo Powell knows he was there and she's not the type of person to lie for nobody. Nord Evans, Mike Perry, no man on the crew is going to lie for Ronny, or Dad, or nobody. You guys don't realize this. You were city raised. These are country folks. Our families have a history here. Our word is gold. That's all we have. We don't lie. In my opinion, you've wasted a lot of time and money going in the wrong direction."

"What do you think should happen to the person who did this shooting?"

"Hell I don't know. Have you listened to anything I've been telling you?"

Detective Ringsage failed to react. He started to ask another question. "Everyone involved in this investigation, except your brother, has cooperated fully and passed their polygraph...."

Johnny didn't let him finish. "My cousin Mark took a lot of psychology courses in college. He told me a habitual liar can pass those tests no sweat because they really believe they're telling the truth."

"The polygraph has been around for over a hundred years," countered Detective Ringsage. "It's about 97 percent accurate."

"Mark says more like 50 percent."

"What I can tell you is the polygraph is like any other tool that has been developed over time. It has gotten better. When I first started, you might be right, but the training an examiner goes through is extensive, and the accuracy now approaches 100 percent. Don't take my word for it. Look it up. I wish that Ronny would have done better, and we could move on, look somewhere else.... Now, I've just got a few more questions and then I'll let you get on with your business of the day. What type of person do you think would commit this offense?"

"You've already asked me that," said Johnny with an exasperated sign. "I don't know the answer, but I will tell you this, my cousin Russell was up there hunting and when it came out you guys were investigating Ronny he was really hot about it. He said he hunted all deer season with Ronny and he was no different than he's always been. If Ronny killed somebody, he'd have been plum different. Ronny is too much like me, shit, if I killed somebody I'd have a nervous breakdown. Hell, here's Ronny, he's quit drinking for over a year now, has been trying to quit smoking and he's kind of off and on that, but he's really working to make everything go right in his life. This deal comes up. I told him don't you dare let this get under your skin. I try to give him a lot of support because I was one of the ones that got after him and made him quit drinking.

Now I hear you're digging into his past—that's ancient history."

Detective Ringsage changed his body language. He leaned forward and his eyes narrowed. "With a case like this, we see who fits our profile and determine if this person is capable of murder. We look to see if someone gets violent when they drink, if they commit assaults or other crimes. I'm not randomly going out and trying to dig up incriminating evidence on Ronny. He fits our profile. I have to investigate him. That's my job."

John laid his hands flat on the table as if granting an offering of peace. "What I'm telling you is Ronny used to get a little ornery when he was drinking. I know because I've had to straighten him out a time or two. When he's not drinking he's fine. He hasn't even drank a beer in over a year. I don't want this to knock him off the wagon. I don't want to see him go back to drinking because you pushed him over the edge. Can't you back off?"

"We have to do what we have to do—just like you," said Detective Ringsage. "You're a good logger, but our job is to investigate crimes and go where the investigation leads us. Right now that leads us to focusing this investigation on Ronny. Now if we were to receive other information.... Tell me this, what reason do you think a person might have for shooting Phil if it wasn't an accident. What reason could there be?"

"Drug drop, maybe."

"Have you ever seen anyone dropping drugs?"

"I'm just going off what happened west of Mitchell, the White Powder Ranch, where they were dropping drugs. That was the first thing I thought of, we got another goddamn outfit dropping drugs, and maybe they sent someone in there to pick up a package, or maybe someone didn't drop what they were suppose to drop. Who knows?"

"This is a two part question. Let's say, theoretically, you accidentally shot Phillip. Would you come forward right away?"

"Hell yes."

"Same question, theoretical, if Ronny had accidentally shot someone, would he come forward?"

"You really didn't want to know how I'd react, you want to know how Ronny would react. Well, the answer is the same. That's the way we were raised."

"Tell me, who would you list as a good suspect?"

"You guys already cleared Clyde Tankersley. Everybody in Wheeler County says he did it. They still say that. They don't care what you say. Personally, I have no use for drug dealers. I'm pretty red neck that way."

"We were definitely very interested in Clyde. We brought him in and he fully cooperated. He did good, real good. So we had to move on. That's what we're doing, getting good people, bring them in and moving on. So, John, do you have anything you want to add?"

"Just that I know my brother, and he didn't do this. If he had, he'd be back drinking and everything else. He couldn't keep it bottled up inside of him. That's all I've got to say."

⊕ ⊕ ⊕

Otho Caldera, citing health issues, resigned as Wheeler County Sheriff and Craig Ward, the gunslinging lawman, the Buffalo Bill look alike and former member of the two-man Portland possum patrol, was appointed to fill out Otho's term. He was now up for election, and to impress the locals and win their votes, he appeared at a Mitchell City Council meeting to discuss the intricacies of the ongoing Phil Brooks homicide investigation. He prefaced his remarks by saying he was not going to mention names, but everyone in attendance knew whom he was talking about. The ranch adjacent to the Fopiano was, of course, the Sixshooter. The *old guy* was Nord Evans. And the *young guy* was Ronny Rhoden. What Craig Ward did not know was that all proceedings of the Mitchell City Council were taped and part of the public record.

"What I wanted to speak to you about this evening is the Phil Brooks homicide investigation. There have been some comments around the community on what is happening. We have never officially spoken to you about the incident and subsequent investigation. The reason for that is homicide is the most serious crime there is, and they can be very delicate cases to prosecute. We have found through experience that the less said the better. Every time we share information in a public venue we run the risk of having that come back and haunt us when we eventually go to trial. This evening I want to walk that very fine line between giving you as much information as I can, and not crossing over the line and jeopardizing the case, which is very much an active one.

"I will begin by explaining that Phil worked that morning at his regular ranch job. He asked his employer to take the afternoon off to work with a green broke colt that belonged to his sister. I mention that because one rumor I constantly hear is that Phil was ambushed, and I think that is highly unlikely because nobody, not even Phil, knew where he was going to be, or when he was going to be there. It would have been impossible for someone to set up and deliberately ambush Phil.

"He rode past the reservoir and commenced to proceed in a northwesterly direction. He ended up on this finger ridge, directly south of Bearway Meadow. He commenced to ride west down this finger ridge. At some point his horse spooked and in fact he broke a rein. The most logical summarization is that some elk broke out of this canyon and ran in front of him and spooked the horse. This area was lousy with elk and elk sign. He managed to regain control of the horse and rode until he dismounted from his horse. He held the reins in one hand and squatted down in this manner, hunkered on his heels. He had the reins in his left hand and a snuff can in his right. He took a chew of snuff. That was probably his last act on earth. At that point he received a high-velocity rifle round in the chest, at a straight on direction. It was instantly fatal. It penetrated his heart and he fell backwards.

"When Phil did not return that evening the word went out and the assumption was that Phil, who was an accomplished horseman and in superb physical condition, was in trouble. So, friends commenced to search. The Wheeler County Sheriff's Office was notified mid-afternoon. When we got out there, literally hundreds of searchers were already in the field—on foot, on horseback, on ATVs, jeeps, and flying airplanes. They were all looking for Phil. At that particular point, nobody expected foul play. We assumed this green broke horse had thrown Phil and that he had broken his hip, or maybe even his neck. He had been gone for more than 24 hours. We knew it was serious.

"That evening the search managers tried to decide the best way to deploy our assets. We felt it best to get an extremely competent tracking team in there at first light. The volunteers had done an excellent job of basically covering specific areas sufficiently enough that we thought Phil was not in those areas. On the other hand, the search was extremely unorganized in the early stages, and we were working with people who had various levels of skill in the search process. The problem we had was so many people had been in there, the tracks were contaminated.

"The search crew we chose is comprised of a professional team out of the Warm Springs Indian Reservation. They arrived about 3 or 4 o'clock the next morning and we had them in near Bearway Meadow before first light. They backtracked Phil's horse that was found in Bearway Meadow and basically they walked right up to his body. At that point, it became apparent we did not have an accident; we had a homicide and that changed the complexion of the situation significantly.

"Homicide in the United States of America has an arrest and conviction rate in excess of 90 percent. Which means law enforcement solves almost all homicides. Most homicides are not difficult to solve. The chances are if anybody in this room is murdered, you will be murdered at the hand of your spouse, or a relative, or friend. The key phrases in a homicide case is that if you find the motive, you find the murderer.

"Homicide has such a high clearance rate because somebody is always watching, even in the biggest city and the darkest alley. These days someone is probably video taping it. However, that does not apply to the case of the Phil Brooks homicide.

This was a very remote, rural location and there were no eyewitnesses around so that complicated things.

"Most homicides are conducted at extremely close range, which gives us blood spatter, footprints, fingerprints, fiber and hair transfer, physical evidence that is helpful in solving the crime. In this particular instance, the murderer never approached the body. I will not tell you how far away the gunshot was fired from, but suffice to say it was at an extreme enough distance there was absolutely no transfer of physical evidence whatsoever in this case. The location where the suspect fired from was an area that was completely contaminated in the early stages of the search.

"Something that got our investigative team the most excited was in finding camping equipment in a dry creek bed. This turned out to be the Californian bow hunters. One of these individuals owns an archery shop down in the San Francisco Bay area. He goes around the western United States and assists people who are trying to do a fee hunting lease rights operation and consults with them on how to set it up and he takes video footage and then he will promote that down in California. He had done this three years previously for the individual who had the rights leased on the Collins Ranch. But then what he did, he and his buddy, was to come up here and hunt without benefit of paying the fee.

"The two bow hunters camped on Buckpoint Road and rode a two-wheel ATV to the ranch, went under a cable gate and hid it and hiked into the area. Phil was already dead by then. We have run their alibi down exhaustively, and among other things they have a receipt from a truck stop in Redding, California and bought a pair of binoculars at exactly the time Phil was being killed. So we know they didn't kill him. However, the information they gave to us is extremely useful and I will show you how it comes into play here in a few minutes.

"So, we managed to clear the Californians and the camping equipment. Incidentally, we polygraphed them and they both passed with flying colors. We have polygraphed an awful lot of people in this case. This is the most exhaustive case I've ever been involved with in my life. Ordinarily a homicide police report will fit in a three ring binder. This case now takes up more than an entire file drawer. We have run every possible lead that has come in to us. The man-hours are incredible.

"What we look at are means, opportunity, motive and jeopardy. As to means, very few people were authorized to be up in there on the Fopiano. A barbed wire fence marks the boundary between the Fopiano Ranch and the Sixshooter Ranch to the north. The Sixshooter had several logging crews operating in the area. The primary logging crew was located about a mile from where Phil was killed—two members of that crew, a young guy and an old guy, happened to be working with heavy equipment at this rock pit, trying to generate some rocks for the road in the logging operation. I will not, in this dissertation, mention any names. I can't mention any names. There are two reasons I'm not going to mention any names; the first is I'm not 100 percent sure who killed Phil. I'm about 90 percent sure. The second reason is that if I mention names it puts us in a liability situation. I will not sling accusations around.

"These two individuals I will tell you about, were the closest individuals to the situation, but they were running heavy equipment so they wouldn't have heard any shots. But one of those individuals, the young guy, claimed he heard a shot in a particular time frame. This is of interest because this was after Phil was already dead, and at that point the Californians were on the property. These bow hunters did not hear a shot. But this young guy claims he heard a shot. This gives us great pause, along with other evidence, to question the veracity of the statements of this particular individual.

"These two bow hunters are up there trying to poach themselves a trophy elk and all of a sudden there are planes and the ground is full of horseman and people on ATVs beating back and forth through the brush. These guys think, holy smokes if these guys catch us they're gonna kill us because they hate trespassers. That is why these guys got out of there as quickly as they could. So much for the Californians.

"We've looked at numerous other people as possible suspects in this slaying. There was an individual down in Spray who had had some harsh words, and in fact a physical altercation with Phil in the months previous to his murder. This individual was looked at very thoroughly, and his alibi is absolutely confirmed by numerous individuals in Spray. We also polygraphed him and there was no doubt he was telling the truth.

"We have polygraphed more people in this case than any case I have been on in my 23 years in this business. A polygraph is useful and is as much science as it is art. About 50-50. It is a very accurate machine, but it is operator dependent, and so in order for a polygraph to be accurate, you have to have an extremely unbiased and competent operator. Thirty-seven states currently accept polygraphs as evidence. Oregon is one of the 13 that does not. So to us a polygraph is a very useful investigative tool, but we can't use the information we extract in a court of law.

"Because of the proximity of the logging crew to the crime scene, we interviewed them very quickly, except for the two gentlemen who were at the rock pit. That gave us pause later in the investigation. These individuals were not made available to us until later in the investigation. We were allowed to speak to everyone in this logging crew. But the young guy who was working on the heavy equipment spoke with us very freely at first, and we had no reason to doubt him and the statements he was making to us. However, after a while, some of the things he said began to create questions and concerns in our minds as to the veracity of what he was telling us.

"Ultimately we scheduled a polygraph examination and that individual, in simple terms, he flunked, flunked badly. Polygraph is seldom black and white. Ordinarily it is shades of gray. The way it works is the examiner will come out and tell the investigators on question number three the individual shows some deception, or strong deception, but again, his interpretation will be in shades of gray. The particular case examiner who administered the test to the young guy came out and he was astonished because, at that juncture, we had not been looking at this individual as a suspect. His polygraph was simply a routine matter, but this guy flunked this real badly. Given that, we then consulted with the three leading examiners in the state of Oregon and collectively they have like 80 years of experience and are the three most respected examiners in the state. We showed the polygraph tapes to those examiners independently and each came out and said, this man is your killer. I can't take it to court. It is inadmissible as evidence. But this makes it pretty conclusive in my mind as to who the killer is.

"We continued to look into the backgrounds of many people associated with this case. The number of interviews we have conducted approaches the hundreds, and we have investigated possible suspects to the third and fourth layer. At this juncture, we have no suspects except for this one individual, this young guy.

"From time to time rumors have circulated how this was drug connected, or a government conspiracy, or all sorts of other wild rumors. We have run down each and every rumor, gone so far as to get satellite image photographs, radar tracking, flight plans and to try and track down a black helicopter and fixed wing airplane doing a parachute drug drop. Folks, let me tell you here tonight, not one shred of credible evidence to support those contentions is available, or makes any sense. These rumors are fantasy. Pure fantasy.

"We are searching for a reason someone felt compelled to kill Phil Brooks; no matter how twisted that reason might be we will search until we uncover that reason. I believe the reason will be much more prosaic than most people believe. I am satisfied that some individual, and I'm not saying who, knew of the elk in this immediate location—as any rancher knows an elk does not respect fences and they will cross back and forth—but this individual I am speaking about knew the location of the elk and he went over the fence to either spook the elk back over the fence, or maybe to get a look at them, but more than likely to start the season a little early. Otherwise, why would this young guy carry a high-powered rifle? You wouldn't if you were going to look at elk, or haze them back onto your property.

"This individual was moving in a southerly direction, across Bearway Meadow and Phil saw him coming for a ways. I think Phil squatted down to watch and when this person came within a certain distance, Phil confronted him. I believe this individual, in an instant, formulated the intent to do what he did. When Phil confronted this person the individual knew he was dirty, knew he was trespassing, a Class A Misdemeanor. This young guy we are looking at has been in significant trouble in the past, and he didn't want any more trouble with the law. He panicked, spun around and fired the rifle that fast. There are a lot of specific scenarios about how that happened, but I am personally, absolutely, satisfied that this is what happened. Do not think that this was an accidental shooting, or that someone mistook Phil for an elk. I think it was a deliberate shooting, not an ambush, but something far simpler, something reactionary.

"What do we need to take this to court? The standard to prove a case like this is beyond a reasonable doubt, a legal concept that basically says a jury must be convinced to a reasonable certainty that this guy did it. In numerical terms this is 96 percent to 98 percent positive this person committed the crime. As a juror, in no case are you ever 100 percent sure. There is always that remote chance that aliens from the planet Zordoc came down here and killed Phil Brooks. But it is just not very likely.

"Those of you who followed the blood and fiber transfer in the O.J. Simpson case know the evidence was absolutely overwhelming, and yet the prosecution failed to convince the jury beyond a reasonable doubt. If we had one-tenth of the evidence here that they had in the O.J. trial, I think we could carry this case. But at this point we don't.

"What qualifies as evidence? There is physical evidence. It could be blood spatter, a footprint, a glove.... We don't have any of that in this case. What we do have, I am not going to tell you. The second thing a case can be built around are eyewitnesses. We don't have eyewitnesses here. All we have is the killer and the guy who died. The third thing an investigator tries to obtain to build a case is a confession. We don't have a confession in this case. We came awfully close. At the conclusion of the young guy's polygraph, this individual was interviewed for some considerable length and we were oh so close to having him confess, but at the last minute he locked up and won't do it. As law enforcement officials we have certain parameters in which we must operate when it comes to interviewing. For instance, eight hours of interrogation is pretty extensive and if it had gone on for twelve hours the court might have taken a hard look at that, even though we gave this individual plenty of breaks, soda pop and food.

"There is no point in rushing this, and pressing for an arrest because of the double jeopardy rule. That means the state cannot bring the same charges against any individual on the same crime more than once. We have one shot to make our case. If we go to court now, and for some reason we lose it, we could never charge this young guy again with Phil's death. Even if subsequently we had a confession, or an eyewitness was to step forward, we could not bring him to trial a second time. And so, we have to wait until we have solid evidence to tie him to this crime. Most crimes have a statue of limitations, which means if an individual is not charged within a certain amount of time, the state cannot charge them. Homicide is an exception. There is no statute of limitations on the crime of homicide. If it takes 20 years to crack the case, so be it. At that time we will bring the charges and try the case.

"Nobody is giving up on this case. In fact, I spoke with Detective Ringsage today and he is the first to confirm this is still very much an active case. But with that said, as officers of the law we must confine ourselves to operating within the bounds of the law. Those are the rules we have given an oath to abide by and we must.

"A couple of things that have caused me concern with the particular individual we are dealing with is why would he, if he knew he was dirty, agree to take a polygraph test. Turns out this individual got in some serious trouble about 15 years ago and one thing he did at that time was to hire his own polygraph examiner. He passed the box. Remember, I said the results are highly operator dependent and there are some unscrupulous independent polygraph operators who will essentially give you the results you want. It all depends on how the questions are formulated and how they are interpreted. I feel that was what happened in that case. Bottom line is, the guy beat the box once before, and he thought he could beat the box again.

"Another problem I have is with the co-worker, the old guy who was with him. The thing that raises my eyebrows is that this individual worked for this operation for many, many years. He is an avid hunter, and in all those years he was never allowed to hunt that ranch. But this fall, after the homicide, he was allowed to hunt the ranch. That could be coincidental, but I have my strong doubts that it is."

At that point Sheriff Craig Ward asked the crowd if they had any questions. A woman in the front row wanted to know whether the old guy had taken a polygraph. The sheriff answered that he refused and went on to say that in the early stages of the investigation law enforcement had been allowed to freely roam the adjacent ranch. But after the young guy had flunked his polygraph, law enforcement was no longer welcome on the property and the only way they could go in to search the brush piles and the fishing ponds for the murder weapon was with a search warrant.

"So, what you're saying is, unless this young guy marches in and says I'm the dude who done it, he goes scot-free," said another member of the audience. Craig Ward answered that if this individual has a conscious it will eat at him until he confesses.

"I heard someone hired a psychic, is that true?"

The sheriff flashed a mischievous grin and shook his head. "I may not personally be a believer in that sort of thing, but yes, we have been contacted by three psychics. I won't go into detail, but suffice it to say we have attempted to search out the validity of any and all possible leads, no matter where those leads may have been initiated."

⊕ ⊕ ⊕

Tom Cutsforth, the Wheeler County District Attorney, placed a call to the Brooks family. What he had to tell Joyce Brooks sent her into a state of depression, and when Jim came in from irrigating, he found her sitting at the kitchen table beside the memorial to their dead son, and she was sobbing into a dishtowel.

"It took a while but finally Joyce come around and told me what had her so goddamn upset," said Jim. "Seems Cutsforth called to say Ronny Rhoden had murdered Phil and the state police were gonna arrest him. He promised he'd try him for murder, and if he got the verdict he planned to get, he'd go for the death penalty.

"That didn't make no sense to me, why this son-of-a-bitch, out of the clear blue, would call up and tell us what he was gonna do. Cops don't do that shit. I said somethin' ain't right here, and told Joyce not to believe everythin' that goofy bastard had to say. Cutsforth he ain't all that sharp, not in my book anyway. I had him figured. What he wants is to push me over the edge, have me to go off my rocker, shoot Ronny, which is exactly what I'd do if I knew for sure he was the one killed Phil.

"I told Joyce, if they got somethin' solid to hang on Ronny they'd already have him locked away. They wouldn't be goin' around makin' idle threats they was gonna arrest him. And I say it's damn stupid to call up here and say somthin' like that. Then I went back outside to finish my irrigatin'. I ain't got time to waste on a fuckin' DA who's got his head wedged so far up his ass he can't wiggle his ears."

After Jack Rhoden learned the district attorney had called the Brooks family and claimed Ronny's arrest was imminent, he called Jim Brooks and asked if he could come over in the morning, said he had some things they needed to talk over. Jim said that was fine with him.

"Mom called and said Jack Rhoden was coming to their house in the morning," said Tina Bolton. "She was all anxious and worried. I told her Wendy and I would be there, and for her to just settle down. As soon as I hung up with Mom, I called an attorney and asked his advice. He told me we might have our suspicions, but that no family member should ever publicly say we think a particular person killed Phil, not unless we could prove it. He also advised me to call the state police and let them know about this latest development."

Tina did call Detective Ringsage and informed him about the scheduled meeting. He said he was surprised, given the circumstances, that Jack would ever set foot on the Brooks' property. He encouraged Tina to take notes and write down everything Jack said. When Tina asked if she could use a tape recorder he said it was illegal to tape a conversation unless all the principals agreed. The following morning, Tina and Wendy were up at 4 a.m. and driving to Mitchell. They waited in the living room with their mother while Jim sat alone at the kitchen table.

"Jack got to the house around nine," recalled Jim Brooks. "I asked him if he'd like a cup of coffee or a cold beer. He said he wasn't thirsty but asked if he could smoke. I got him an ashtray. His hands were shakin' when he lit his cigarette and when he started talkin' his voice was breakin' up. I felt bad for him. I knew he was all tore up inside."

Between nervous puffs on his cigarette, Jack explained that on the afternoon Phil had been killed, his boy Ronny had come to the office in Prineville. Jack said he was having oral surgery the following day and Ronny had come to take care of some business and to see him off. He admitted his youngest son had been in trouble in the past, but he defended him, saying he hadn't had anything to drink in over a year and that he had been doing real well. He claimed there was no way Ronny could have killed Phil and invited Jim to talk to the guys on the logging crew and they would tell him the truth.

"Jack talked for a half hour or so," recalled Jim. "It seemed like he was tryin' to convince himself that his boy didn't do it. He never convinced me. After he got done I thanked him. I told him it took a lot of guts for him to come see me like he did. I respect Jack for doin' that. As far as his boy goes, if he didn't do it, why can't they clear his name?"

⊕ ⊕ ⊕

"When the DA called, one of the things he told Mom was the Warm Springs trackers had followed Ronny Rhoden's footprints from the logging site all the way to the crime scene and back to the logging site," stated Tina Bolton. "When I related that information to Robb Ringsage he really fired off and said he didn't know where the DA was getting his information. It wasn't true. Why would Cutsforth come out and say something like that?"

⊕ ⊕ ⊕

Two years after Phil Brooks' death, Keith Baker, the Warm Springs tracker who found Phil's body, was still haunted by the unresolved case. He wanted to see firsthand what he had been going over in his mind, trying to piece together what had happened, how it had happened and why it happened. Jim Walker, reserve Wheeler County Sheriff's Deputy, accompanied Keith and several members of his tracking team onto the Fopiano.

Keith and Jim were standing at the spot known as *the long shot* and Keith said he was now even more convinced than ever that Phil had not been shot from this location. The trees had grown taller and wider and the window of visibility had shrunk to a narrow slit between the tightly packed trees. Keith said, "I lost all respect for Ringsage when he focused his attention on *the long shot* and excluded any other possibility.

"The first time I saw him flustered was right here. We argued about *the long shot*. I said it wasn't possible, and was trying to spell out all the reasons why this could not be the shooter. Ringsage refused to listen. But another officer, who was standing there, said I had some solid arguments and Ringsage might be wrong. Ringsage stuttered and stammered—he did that anytime he got flustered or mad—and he started screaming at me. I took a step back. I addressed the other officer and calmly told him, 'You best get a leash on your dog; he's out of control.'"

This infuriated Detective Ringsage all the more and he made an aggressive move toward Keith. He shouted he had spent years investigating with the state police and Keith had no clue what was going on. He said he could throw Keith off the search scene and have him arrested for hindering prosecution.

"You stupid son-of-a-bitch," barked Keith. "I don't work for you. I work for Otho Caldera."

After Keith challenged Detective Ringsage, Keith said, "The man stormed off stomping his feet like a little kid who didn't get his way."

Jim Walker had his own run-ins with Detective Ringsage, most centered on Mike Williams as a possible suspect. He said, "When I started putting the case together by time and date, I got to looking and asked, 'Why has nobody ever looked at Mike Williams? Why hasn't he taken a lie detector test?'

"When I reread the notes and saw Mike Williams had changed what he told the state police, that his alibi didn't hold water, that he had constantly interjected himself into the investigation like a guilty man will do, that his rifles had never been checked and he had never taken a polygraph, I tried to push the issue. But I could never touch Mike Williams, couldn't touch the son-of-a-bitch. I was told to drop it. I had no choice. I dropped it."

Once again, as they had done two years before, Keith and Jim explored *the short shot* and the brush pile, where the suspected shooter had run to and where that person had a pickup parked. Here they made a startling discovery.

"I found fresh boot prints. What shocked me was that the tracks were made by the same individual I had followed on *the short shot* two years before," said Keith. "The stride was the same, indicating an injury to the right upper leg. This person walked heavy on the left foot. The right foot turned out. What did that mean? To me it meant the person I suspected was the shooter still had access to the property two years after the murder. What business did they have there? I didn't know. Who did I suspect? It would be purely supposition on my part, but it would have to be someone with unlimited access to this property, then and now."

Another tie-in to the suspected shooter was the fresh tracks led to where a pickup truck had been parked beside the brush pile, the same as after the murder. And once again the tire tracks matched—Les Schwab Wild Country tires—the identical tread pattern Keith had recorded and that had been photographed after the murder.

"But we found more," related Keith. "We climbed onto the bench behind where Phil was killed, where his horse had been running. I had never been to that area before. It was where Phil had come from, where he must have ridden the day he was killed, and it was here we found a bone yard. Someone, over a number of years, had waylaid elk at this site. Nine piles of elk bones were located, they were of varying age and each was missing the head, except for one and this skull had been cut with a saw, a distinctive V-shape cut, to remove the horns. What we had was a killing field."

Jim Walker alerted Detective Ringsage to this unusual discovery, and two weeks later nine uniformed officers, as well as Jim Walker, Keith Baker and members of the Warm Springs tracking team visited the scene to collect evidence. The problem was, the night before their arrival the first storm of the year had blanketed the area under a dusting of fresh snow.

"I had marked where the bone piles were," said Jim Walker. "But when I brushed the snow away the bones were gone. And when we couldn't find the bones the state cops dicked us around, made like we were stupid assholes—kinda like here are two fat boys and their Indian tracking team and la-la-la-la—they threw what I called a haphazard investigation and that was it, man. They had metal detectors and were trying to find a bullet in the trees. Crazy, like looking for a needle in a haystack. I don't know why the state police treated us the way they did. I guess they were frustrated and took it out on us."

CHAPTER 6

Misdirection

A cream colored VW bus swooped into Central Oregon with cute flower decorations painted around the windows, looking for all the world like a goddamn hippy van a couple decades late for the big love in. But the unique thing about this bus was painted on the rear door panel, a logo of a blue moon and the words "Bounty Hunter." Behind the wheel was Chung; tall and thin, with platinum hair, skin as white as an albino and peculiar eyes that could change without warning from soft blue to a menacing shade of red. He claimed to be a mercenary and his brag was he had arrived in town to solve the Phil Brooks homicide, bring the killer to justice and collect the $65,000 reward.

Chung was born Dale Kielhorn in 1951. He grew up south of The Dalles, Oregon on a hardscrabble farm 10 miles after the pavement turned into a dirt road. His father ran the liquor store in The Dalles and drove to work five days a week while his son ran wild in the hills, hunting, fishing and tending a trap line. When Dale was in his teens the family moved to the Willamette Valley, near the town of Gaston, and Dale attended the strict Seventh Day Adventist Laurelwood School. Upon graduating from high school, Dale went to work in the woods, setting chokers and high lead, until Uncle Sam intervened and served him with a draft notice in 1968. After basic training, Dale was shipped to Vietnam where he served two tours as a Dust-Off medic on a helicopter crew. When he came home in 1971, the war had changed him. He just wasn't right in the head.

He escaped back into the woods and lived in a remote logging camp where his contact with people was limited to those men he worked with. Then he got hurt, took his medical payoff in cash, and caught a flight to Japan where he spent a couple years teaching English to Japanese students. He returned to the Northwest, went back to work in the woods, saved his money, and after gathering another grubstake, flew to Australia. This time, when his money ran low he came home, enrolled in college at Eastern Oregon University where he said he earned a degree in Economics. Then, according to Dale, he got married, but his wife died suddenly of toxic shock syndrome and after that his life went into an out of control tailspin.

Dale was supposedly diagnosed with Post Traumatic Stress Disorder, a reaction to the trauma he faced in the war, and the army awarded him 100 percent disability. Dale, who had a hard time finishing a thought to a logical conclusion without whirling off on a confusing tangent, said, "In my case I did a phenomenal amount of combat: landings in live zones and saw hundreds of our soldiers dead. It adds up. Gives you a stress anxiety level. The government told me I was unemployable. But I'm motivated. I went to Portland State University. Earned a masters degree in Public Administration and was accepted into the PHD program. Nineteen times I went to be interviewed for government jobs and they won't hire me. They said my condition had gotten worse. I took an elective course in Tae Kwondo. Trained for nine months, got my black belt and won the National Tae Kwondo Heavyweight Championship in 1991."

There is no record of Dale having attended any of the colleges he said he attended, and he was not the National Tae Kwondo Heavyweight Championship in 1991. When he showed up in Central Oregon he was living in his hippy van and looking for a way to earn a living. He was tall, maybe 6 foot 5 and built for supple quickness, like a greyhound or a whippet. He wore white ballet slippers because he said they made him look fast on his feet, and he tended to stare at people with those vacant and unnerving blue-red eyes that seemed to be missing some essential human quality. When he stopped in Mitchell and started asking questions about Phil Brooks, he alarmed most folks.

"I was working collecting gambling debts and protection money for the Portland Mafia, but I got out of that," claimed Dale. "My Tae Kwondo instructor gave me the name Chung. It means blue in Korean. Chung is a man to fear. Chung travels all over the world looking for bounties. Chung stopped in Prineville and the receptionist at the forest service office told Chung about Phil Brooks and the reward. She said she had known Phil. She began to cry. Chung was touched in his heart. Chung promised to bring the murderer to justice and right this terrible wrong."

⊕ ⊕ ⊕

Tom Parker was a carpenter and in the fall of 1995 he was building a hunting cabin for Mike and Roetta Williams on the Fopiano Ranch. The generator was running and Tom was busy cutting a sheet of plywood with a skill saw. He thought he was alone.

"Suddenly there's a pair of white slippers—about size 15— right next to me and I look up and this tall dude, with white skin and long, stringy blonde hair, is staring down at me with the weirdest eyes I've ever seen. Kid you not, he puts the fear of God in me," said Tom. "I shut off the generator. This guy tells me his name is Chung, and he rambles on about his having done three tours in Nam, says he's killed more gooks than Carter has liver pills, that he fears no man, and he talks about how he is going to bring the man who murdered Phil Brooks to justice. He wants to know what I know about the case. I tell him he needs to talk to Mike Williams.

"This guy is very aggressive in his mannerism. There is just something totally unsettling about this guy. He is like a stick of dynamite with the fuse lit and I'm just waiting for it to explode. He intimidates me big time. I tell him Mike knows a state policeman and he has all the information about what happened and the caliber of the rifle that killed the kid, and I tell him he should come back when Mike is around. I'm basically trying to get rid of the guy.

"Then he starts talking about martial arts and tells me to stick out my hand. I do and he flips me onto my back so fast I don't even know what happened. I'm laid out flat. This guy is towering over me, smiling and I fail to see any humor in the situation. I don't much want to get up, but I do. I go to the cooler, pull out a can and offer this crazy man a beer. He takes it, drinks it, claims Jimmy Collins gave him the combination to the gate; that he can go wherever he wants to go and all I do is agree with him and hope he leaves and leaves in a hurry. This guy is spooky—I kid you not—real bad spooky."

⊕ ⊕ ⊕

Chung wheeled his VW bus—a shrunken human head dangling and swaying from the mirror—past the Fossil city limit sign. Chung parked and walked into the Fossil Café. He announced in an alarmingly loud voice he was a bounty hunter, and began firing questions at patrons concerning the Phil Brooks homicide. He demanded answers.

Reserve Deputy Jim Walker, who was cooking at the café, came out from the kitchen with an apron tied around his waist and challenged Chung, demanding to know if Chung had any weapons.

"I am a weapon," hissed Chung.

Holding his ground Jim asked, "Do you have a gun?" Chung said he did not. And after the face-off the two men began talking, and when Chung said he had served in Vietnam, Jim said he had too, and the men, having found common ground, relaxed and began visiting. Jim agreed to meet Chung the following day and advised Chung to refrain from asking any more questions about Phil Brooks and the homicide investigation. He said some of the locals might take exception to an out-of-town bounty hunter stirring up the pot.

The following day the two men met in the sheriff's office, and since the investigation seemed to be stalled, Walker agreed to work with Chung. He told him what he knew about the investigation while withholding the sensitive information that was not to be released to the public. After that meeting, Chung drove to Prineville and made copies of all the stories about the murder that were in the newspapers. He talked to the Crook County sheriff, who mentioned Detective Robb Ringsage was the lead investigator in the case. Chung called the state police headquarters and arranged a meeting with Detective Ringsage.

"Ringsage gave me nothing," lamented Chung. "And then he went around behind my back and poisoned the well with the Brooks family. He told them I was a kook because he didn't want me to solve the case. Every time I turned around I found where Robb Ringsage had suppressed evidence. I was told he had everything he needed to make an arrest in the case, but he was afraid of power and afraid of money, afraid he might jeopardize his reputation in the law enforcement community.

"Rather than try and plow the same ground the police had plowed, I decided to go in a completely different direction. I met with Jimmy Collins, and at first we had a standoff. He didn't know what to think of my slippers and dark sunglasses and me driving a bounty hunter VW bus. But we got to visiting and he told me he had been in World War II, was a fighter pilot, and I told him about my experiences in Vietnam. Suddenly we were long-lost buddies. He gave me the combination to the gate and told me where to find the scene of the murder. He didn't show me where to go. He wanted me to find it on my own. I had to prove myself and that was fine with me.

"It took me two full days to find where Phil was killed. And when I did, I felt pretty excited actually. There were red ribbons everywhere and a wooden cross was tacked to a tree. I stood there and it was hallowed ground, where a crime against Mother Earth had been committed. It was very, very sacred to me.

"When you are with someone who dies there is a strange silence that penetrates you. I have seen men die in the woods, seen the enemy die in the jungle and always there is this quiet and the release of a solemn energy, a very low vibration emanates from the ground. I am not sure if being a witness to death makes you more, or if it makes you less; whether it gives you strength, or it robs strength from you. Personally, I feed off the energy of death. People look at me and that is what they see. I am the energy, the vibration of death. And although Phil left this earth, his organic radioactive energy remained. I laid on the ground where Phil died and felt him reach down from the sky, the soft tentacles of his being reaching out to touch me and I became one, united, fused to him in the brotherhood of the spirit world.

"Chung took a rock from that spot where Phil had been, gave it to a psychic and she held it in her hands and said it was like holding a glowing ember. She handed it back, closed off the channel and refused to allow the evil forces from the dark side to reach the light of day. But Chung is not fearful. Chung has no human emotion; compassion, remorse, sympathy, guilt, desire, love. The reward money is the only force that drives Chung. He needs to find a sponsor to help defray his expenses. When someone gives him money he will solve the case, collect the reward and he will have credibility and be loved across the land. Chung wants money. Chung needs money."

The roving bounty hunter went on to say he had tried to contact Bill Smith, the developer from Bend and administrator of the $65,000 reward fund, asking to be reimbursed for a tire and rim he destroyed driving on Waterman Road. Bill Smith never returned his call. And Chung said it was his belief the killer was still in possession of the murder weapon because in the world of oriental arts the weapon was considered the extension of the user and to destroy a weapon would be to destroy a part of oneself. He said ego was involved in the killing of Phil Brooks, and concluded by smiling and saying, "It is one thing to kill a trophy elk, it is quite another to kill a man."

Without funding to continue his search for the killer, Chung went to work at the Rainbow Market, the stop nearest to the Warm Springs Indian Reservation where beer and wine were sold. He was employed as a box boy, but claimed he was actually an undercover bouncer, hired to keep in check some of the unsavory characters lurking in the shadows.

Leaning a shoulder against the beer cooler in the Rainbow Market, Chung said, "Clues are like hunting for mushrooms. You wander for a long time and then you spot one mushroom and generally there are more in the same area and maybe you've already stepped over some and never saw them. Then you go on and you might see more mushrooms hanging in a tree and you have to constantly be looking. And that is the way it is with this case because about the time I think I've exhausted all my leads something new comes along and the clues are all around me. Right now I'm looking into a crime syndicate and prostitution ring, selling kids on the black market, drugs, weapons, and all of it is coming out of Canada and headed to the market in California. Central Oregon is a convenient midpoint drop-off. That's what I'm thinking. Phil came upon something he wasn't supposed to see."

Chung was eventually fired from his job as a box boy because he became overly aggressive with the "under the bridge crew," the group of local alcoholics who hung out around the Rainbow Market, panhandling money to buy more booze that they drank at the boat landing or under the bridge that crosses the Deschutes River. Chung's final act as a bounty hunter, before he abandoned the case, was to write a letter to Oregon Attorney General, Ted Kulongoski in which he bemoaned the arrogant attitude of the Oregon State Police and specifically named Detective Ringsage for his lack of cooperation. The letter stated, "The problem is that Mr. Ringsage uses any information he gets to sabotage my investigation as a bounty hunter. And he has threatened other agencies to back off and butt out. Mr. Ringsage has broken confidences with me on several occasions to the extent that I no longer will trust his legitimacy as an OSP officer. Formally speaking I do not want him near anyone remotely involved in this case. If I ever see or hear of Detective Ringsage following me or harassing the people I talk to again, such as he has done, I will contact an attorney and press charges criminally and sue him civilly."

The hand-written letter rambled on for four pages and delved into other unsolved murder cases in Central Oregon, courier planes and black helicopters and suggested that Phil's death was, "caused because he got in the way of a dope deal," and that Chung's investigation had led him to believe that, "this case involves a statewide crime syndicate." The conclusion warned, "The tension brought down over Phil's death is a time bomb, which if something is not done, will explode between Crook County and Wheeler County in the form of a RANGE WAR."

⊕ ⊕ ⊕

Tina Bolton arrived home and found a message on her answering machine that stated, "I am Chung. I am bounty hunter. I wish to speak to you about your deceased brother. I'll be in touch."

The next time Chung called, Tina was home and after visiting with him she invited the bounty hunter to stop over and visit. When he arrived, he talked about the atrocities of war, the power of martial arts and wove in his wild scenarios about Phil being killed by a drug cartel, baby stealers, black helicopters, a Beach Bonanza flying weapons from Canada and all the craziness that was in his disturbed mind. After listening to him for a couple hours, Tina asked him to leave, brusquely telling him to never contact her again. He had frightened her.

⊕ ⊕ ⊕

For a brief time Zack Keys, the self-proclaimed mayor of the ghost town of Richmond, Oregon, became a suspect in the murder of Phil Brooks. His name surfaced in the investigation when a logger voiced a few concerns—suspicions he called them—and those comments became rumors that eventually got back to Detective Ringsage. The logger was interviewed and he said what worried him was the fact Zack was a hard drinker, had stacks of military and mercenary books and magazines, packed around what he called a "Russian sniper rifle" and that he seemed obsessed with the Phil Brooks homicide.

"Zack gets crazy," the logger told Detective Ringsage. "One time he insisted I read a page in a book called *Ninety-Three Confirmed Kills*. I didn't want to read it, but Zack shoved it in my face and told me, 'Read it, you son-of-a-bitch.' I read it. What this section pertained to was the last victim of the sniper's 93 kills, which was a woman who was shot at 900 yards. When I finished reading, Zack was smiling like a cat that ate the canary. He said that was exactly what happened to Phil Brooks. It was like he knew, and what was even more creepy is that Zack keeps a pile of newspaper clippings about the murder on top of his fireplace mantle and said he went to the site where Phil was killed either the day before, or the day after, the kid died. From the way he acts, I think Zack might have had something to do with the murder."

Zack was married to Linda Keys, the Wheeler County Justice of the Peace, although they had not lived together as husband and wife for a number of years. He was a big man with a bushy Fu-Manchu mustache. If he had been drinking, and he usually was, he was oftentimes mouthy, rude, abrasive and could come across as downright scary. Around the Mitchell area, Zack was best known for raising mouflon sheep on his ranch bordering the John Day River. The trophy animals were allowed to wander onto adjacent public lands where hunters often harvested them. This upset the BLM because they did not want non-native animals introduced into the area, and it upset Zack because these hunters were not paying his customary fee of $1,000.

One time Zack confided to a friend about his fee hunting operation, saying, "When a hunter comes to the ranch I try to size him up. If he looks like a sportsman, I tell him to start hunting about 10 o'clock in the morning, climb way up high into the rimrock and that's where he'll find the big boys. But if the hunter looks like he just wants a trophy and doesn't want to work for it, I tell him to show up at daybreak and check around the haystacks."

Detective Ringsage met with Zack at the Fossil Café, and in a rambling interview Zack talked about mouflon sheep, his hunting operation and his theories relating to how and why Phil Brooks was killed. When asked where he was on the afternoon of September 20th, 1994, Zack replied he was positive he had been logging with his sons at the head of Butte Creek. He went on to say, when he heard from his wife that Phil was missing, he had loaded his horse in his trailer and drove to the Fopiano. He planned to help look for Phil, but that was the morning the Indian trackers found Phil's body and Zack seemed truly disappointed he had not been able to participate in the search.

When asked about snipers and any gun related literature he might possess, Zack declared his favorite book of all time was, *Ninety-Three Confirmed Kills* and proudly acknowledged he subscribed to *Guns and Ammo*, *Shooting Times* and *Gun World* and boasted he kept all the back issues. As Zack continued to talk, Detective Ringsage became more and more unsettled about the man's demeanor and his ramblings. In an effort to narrow the focus of the conversation, the detective asked Zack how well he had known Phil Brooks.

"I knew him alright," said Zack, "but I didn't know him near as good as I know his brother, Justin. Hell, I half raised Justin. He dropped out of school in eighth grade; lived with me. I put him to work. I know Jim real well. Him and me spent a lot of time riding in the hills together. Our families go way back."

Detective Ringsage thought Zack was most likely full of hot air, but still this man was not acting appropriately and thinking he might be hiding something, the detective asked Zack to take a polygraph. Zack, puffed up with self-importance and answered, "Hell yes. I'll go on the box."

Zack Keys passed his polygraph without even a hint of deception. Detective Ringsage no longer considered him a suspect.

⊕ ⊕ ⊕

Naomi, the afternoon bartender at the Shamrock, a beer and hard-liquor bar with an attached dining room in Fossil, and known for pouring an honest drink and serving prime rib dinners every Friday night, had a bizarre story to tell. She said she couldn't be sure about the date, but thought it occurred around the time Phil Brooks was murdered.

"It was late in the day. I do remember that," said Naomi. "This guy walks in and he's real nervous and sweaty and scroungy. I though he must be high on something. He wanted a beer. I told him I couldn't serve him."

"Why not?" the man asked.

"You don't seem normal," said Naomi. "Are you high?"

"You afraid of me?"

Naomi glanced down the bar to where a couple of her regulars were nursing their drinks. She turned back toward the stranger, stepped behind the cash register, and said, "No."

"Then why stand behind the register?"

"I always stand here," said Naomi.

"If I tell you the story why I'm this way, all keyed up, will you serve me a drink? I really need one."

When the man said that, Naomi could tell he was lucid and she relented and poured him a beer. She set the beer on the bar in front of the man. He was wearing camo pants; his hands, arms and face were dirty and his hair was stringy. Even from her side of the bar, Naomi could smell his rankness, a combination of sweat and wood smoke, and she guessed he had been camping. In stark contrast to his general appearance, he had on a clean white, sleeveless T-shirt that looked as though he had just slipped it over his head before he came in the bar. He took a long pull of beer and began talking. "I was hunting and this guy was supposed to be my guide, but he didn't come back and his wife said she'd guide me. This was on private property, but the owners don't allow hunting, you have to sneak around. I wanted to kill a trophy bull. We jump these elk. I thought I saw big horns. I took a shot. When I looked through my rifle scope I panicked."

"Why?" asked Naomi.

"It wasn't an elk. It was something else."

"Really."

"Yeah, what a rush. Bet you never had a rush like that."

"What do you mean?" inquired Naomi.

"Adrenalin rush," he said. "You think you just killed a person and it hits you like a semi truck. Such a goddamn, wild-assed rush."

Naomi picked up her order pad and began drawing the man's distinctive tattoo; the image of a girl on his right shoulder that extended onto his bicep. The face was pretty, done in black with green shading and the hair was pale blond. The man noticed Naomi and said in an accusing tone, "You drawing my tattoo?"

"Admiring it," lied Naomi. "I've a broken heart tattooed on my stomach and my daughters' names on my ankle. I'm just doodling."

The phone rang. Naomi went to answer it and when she returned the man was no longer at the bar. She stepped outside to see in which direction he might have gone and looked to see if he was in a vehicle parked on the street, but he was nowhere to be seen. It was as though he had simply vanished.

Several weeks passed, and then one Saturday night Naomi was sitting in the Shamrock drinking with friends. She saw a man come into the bar and although he looked like someone she should know, she couldn't quite place him. She watched him step to the bar and read his lips as he inquired where he might find the other bartender. The bartender pointed in Naomi's direction; he turned, and when he made eye contact with Naomi he put an index finger to his lips and signaled with his other hand as though he was shooting her. Then he turned and walked away without ever having said anything, or having ordered a drink.

Naomi ran it all through her mind. This man had been well dressed. He was muscular and had longish hair pulled back into a ponytail. For several long minutes she could not place him, and then it came to her—he was the man with the tattoo—the one who claimed he killed someone in a hunting accident.

CHAPTER 7

New Suspects

Dave Rouse became the Wheeler County Sheriff in 2000 and one of his first official acts was to take back the stalled Phil Brooks homicide investigation from the Oregon State Police. Because of his dogged determination, and his ability to get rural folks to speak freely, he developed new leads that soon focused on Mike and Roetta Williams as the primary suspects. He served a search warrant on the Williams' residence and eight years after the murder, District Attorney Tom Cutsforth convened a grand jury to hear evidence in the case and to possibly bring forth an indictment.

The Williams' had originally become suspects in the state police investigation because they had access to the property, didn't have an alibi and if they had been caught poaching, or had a fee hunter poaching, they stood to lose their lease on the Collins' property, their sole source of income at that time. But Mike said he thought the only reason his name had ever come up in the investigation was because the state police were diligently going down a list of names trying to eliminate people. Back in 1998 Detective Ringsage had asked Mike if he would submit to a polygraph, as nearly everyone else in the case had been asked to do, and Mike said he supposed he would. And

177

then he flunked the first test. When that happened, the state police were absolutely shocked. Now, in addition to Ronny Rhoden, they had a second individual who had failed the polygraph. At first they thought a polygraph machine malfunction was to blame. They asked Mike to take another test and he agreed to give it a second go.

As it turned out, both tests revealed Mike Williams was lying when he answered no to the question, "Did you kill Phil Brooks?" And on the second test, when he was asked, "Do you know who killed Phil Brooks?" he became so lightheaded he had to be unhooked from the polygraph machine to keep him from passing out.

Lieutenant Lorin Weilacher, state police polygraph examiner, refused to speak directly of Mike Williams' polygraph examination, but he did say if someone were to pass out, or nearly pass out while taking a polygraph, it would be highly unusual. In all his years in the business, he said he had never heard of such a thing happening. When questioned why a person would react that way, the examiner replied, "For a subject to react in that manner would require that subject to have an extremely high level of nervousness, apprehension and fear to a particular question, or a series of questions."

According to Mike, his experiences of taking two polygraph examinations were "terrible" and "mind blowing" and he went on to say, "Your anxiety is high. Normally I'm pretty laid back. But, you know, I'm like anybody, the anxiety levels go up when they start saying you're deceptive and accusing you of murder. Well let me tell you, it rocks your world."

After flunking the polygraph tests, Mike said he didn't tell anyone what had happened, and yet rumors quickly circulated around Central Oregon. It was suggested the state police had leaked the information to incite the rumor mill and Mike, indicating that was probably true, said, "I'm not pissed they did it. The state police have a job to do. They probably wanted to see what would fall from the sky."

After flunking the second polygraph test, Mike and Roetta *"lawyer-ed up,"* refusing to talk to any member of law enforcement, or the media, and directing any requests for interviews, or questions, go through their attorney. The attorney refused to acknowledge any inquiries that came his way, and the state police all but abandoned the case.

⊕ ⊕ ⊕

Tony Conti, one of nearly a hundred witnesses to be served subpoenas, appeared before a Wheeler County grand jury when it was convened in 2002. After being sworn in, Tony sat in a straight-backed wooden chair and faced the grand jury. Tom Cutsforth stood in the center of the courtroom and started through his list of prepared questions. He wanted to know when Tony had been employed at Mountain Country Sporting Goods, a Bend store operated by Mike and Roetta Williams. Tony testified he served as store manager from 1984 until 1986.

"Did you ever go on any hunting or scouting trips with Mike or Roetta Williams?" asked the DA. The answer was, no. Tony offered that the only time he was ever asked to go anywhere with the Williams' was one time on a salmon fishing trip on the Oregon coast.

"Did you order a .280 caliber Mountain Rifle for Mike Williams?"

"Yes," answered Tony. "I believe it was in 1985. Mike asked me to order that rifle. It was fitted with a variable scope and the wooden stock was changed and customized with a matte finish, black synthetic stock."

When Tony was hired to manage the sporting goods store he said he thought his prayers had been answered. It was his dream job, the opportunity to do something he truly loved and get paid to talk to customers about fishing and hunting.

"We had an inventory of guns fronted to us by a national supplier. The invoices were supposed to be paid as the merchandise was sold," said Tony. "At the start, we had a triple-A credit rating. Business was great. We had a steady stream of customers and they were buying."

On the surface the business seemed successful, and profitable. But then gun and ammunition suppliers quit offering the store credit and instead imposed a COD rule, as did the UPS delivery service. Tony saw the red flags and concluded invoices were not being paid in a timely fashion. He started watching more closely to see exactly what was going on behind the scenes.

"Mike was stealing from the store," said Tony bluntly. "He took money out of the till and put it in his pocket, and he traded stock from the store for personal items: to get his bird dog trained, a new set of tires for his pickup, mechanic work done, that sort of thing. He was bleeding the store dry.

"It got to the point where Mike's stepfather, who was bankrolling the operation, came to me, said he was going to kick Mike and Roetta out, and wanted to know if I'd be willing to take over the store. I thought to myself, 'You have got to be kidding me.' The last thing I wanted was to be in the middle of a family fight. I decided to get out. But then Mike wouldn't pay me the wages I had coming. I had to take him to court before he finally settled up."

During Tony's testimony before the grand jury, neither the district attorney nor members of the grand jury, ever asked him about Mike Williams' business practices. Tony said he wished they had because he thought those practices revealed something important about Mike's character. And Tony said he was never asked his opinion on whether or not he thought Mike or Roetta could have been involved in a homicide.

"If they were involved in the killing it would have to be 100 percent accidental," said Tony. "How could a person live with himself, or herself, if they were the one who pulled the trigger? But then again, I ask myself how could a person steal from his parents on a daily basis? If you can swallow the stealing apple, maybe you could choke down murder.... I don't know."

⊕ ⊕ ⊕

Scott Reid, Mike Williams' brother-in-law, was called to testify before the grand jury and according to Scott, "The impression I got was that the DA was looking for someone to hang the blame on, and he decided to hang it on Mike and Roetta. I don't think there's a shred of evidence to tie them to the murder, and what else I think is that unless the cops have some damn solid proof, they shouldn't be accusing them.

"The DA wanted to know if Mike or Roetta were smokers back in 1994 when Phil Brooks got killed. I said they both smoked but since then they kicked the habit and now chew. I'm not sure what flavor Mike prefers but I know Roetta chews Skoal."

The grand jury wanted to know if Mike or Roetta ever packed a rifle when they were bow hunting. Scott said, to the best of his knowledge, they didn't, and went on to relate, when they were guiding, they never packed a rifle. It was strictly up to the hunter to make the kill. When pressed by the district attorney to recall how many times he had hunted with Mike and Roetta, Scott could only recall twice: once when he and Mike went deer hunting up Bear Creek and Mike killed a nice buck, and another time when he and Mike traveled to Wyoming to hunt antelope.

"The other thing they wanted to know about was a .280 rifle," said Scott. "I didn't even know about that gun until all this came up and then I remember overhearing Roetta tell my wife that Mike had given her a custom .280 as a gift. Mike sold the rifle to some guy in Redmond. Mike was always doing that, selling stuff, trading stuff. He had a bill of sale for the rifle. It was all on the up and up."

After he finished testifying, Scott was in a talkative mood. He offered, "They never hardly asked me nothin'. If they had asked, I would have told them Roetta said they weren't even in the country when it happened. On the day the kid was killed she and Mike were in Redmond. That's what she said. And the next day they came over to hunt on private ground and camped right next to Greer Kelly. They didn't even find out about the kid getting killed until the following day.

"I do know this thing's got Roetta all tore up inside. She can't figure out why the cops are harassing them. She says they haven't done nothin' but the cops hound them like they have. When the cops showed up at their house Roetta was fightin' mad, ready to toss them out, but they had a subpoena and a search warrant and she threw up her hands, said, 'Help yourself.' According to what Roetta told my wife, the cops packed in three or four big empty cardboard boxes and all they hauled out was a handful of empty casings, some powder and a few bullets. That was it.

"I don't know how Roetta is gonna handle this situation. Guess she just has to wait and see what develops. But she still has her sense of humor. Just yesterday she was laughing about it and told me, if they haul her off to jail, she wants me to bring her a roll of snuff. She said as long as she has her Skoal they can go ahead and lock her up in jail."

When Scott was asked about Mike and Roetta's relationship he said, "It's like most married folks, they have their ups and downs. They fight and make up. I don't think it comes to blows or anything like that but they do have some pretty good cussing matches. Most of their fights come about 'cause Roetta gets to hittin' the bottle pretty good and that upsets Mike. After they have a blowup Roetta comes over to our house, says Mike did something to piss her off and her nose will be out of joint. But by morning all is fine. Roetta likes her wine. Her daddy was a wino. He died maybe four years ago, flat ass broke. Drank it all up, didn't have a goddamn dime to his name.

"For the most part Mike wears the pants in the family, up to a certain point and then Roetta does. Mike takes care of most of the financial situations—the trading, the buying, the selling—and Roetta runs the household and buys groceries. Mike never has had no money of his own. His stepdad was part owner in a sawmill and he bailed Mike out time after time. But he died and now all Mike has to do is holler, 'Momma' and his mother gives him what he wants.

"You know, my getting called to testify in front of the grand jury put me in a tough position. You gotta swear to tell the truth. There are some family matters I was glad they didn't ask me about 'cause I really didn't want to say anything. For one thing, money has always been a bone of contention between Mike and Roetta. They like to live high on the hog even when they can't afford it. They go through periods were they'll be down and out, and then all of a sudden they're buying more stuff and going great guns. My wife wonders where in the hell Mike is getting his money. I do know it cost them a bunch to put their boy Grant through school to be a paramedic, and they were making his pickup payments, paying his insurance, gas bill and even his phone bill and he was running that up over $300 a month.

"Their daughter, Jennifer, she married a guy named Jason and he is a radical. I don't know if he's mixed up in drugs or not, but he gets drunk and knocks Jennifer around. He steps out on her, too.

"Here just the other day the whole family was camped out in the woods. Mike got into it with Jason. Mike ain't as young as he used to be. He was getting the shit beat out of him and Roetta jumped on Jason's back, trying to protect Mike. Some fellow in another camp came over and had to break it up before someone really got hurt. When Jason was walking away he turned to Mike and called him a 'Murderin' son-of-a-bitch.' And that seemed a little strange, him sayin' a thing like that.

"I think if Roetta was involved in the murder, and I'm not saying she was, but if she was, I think Mike would cover for her to the bitter end. If the tables were turned, Roetta might not do the same for Mike. I've thought about all this, thought about it a lot, and I suppose it's possible they could have had some rich fee hunter in there on the Fopiano hunting illegally. That would be something Mike might do. Like I said, he does like the green stuff.

"The one thing Mike would be worried about was if he did something that might cause him to lose his hunting rights. What he would do to protect them? I don't know. But if it was an accident, and Mike killed the kid, I do believe he'd come forward and admit it like a man."

⊕ ⊕ ⊕

Tom Parker was a carpenter by profession, but he also acted as a big game guide, taking hunters onto private property to hunt for a fee. Tom became friends with Mike Williams and in 1995 they put together a deal where Tom agreed to build a hunting cabin on the Fopiano in return for lifetime hunting privileges.

"The cabin was going to upgrade Mike's operation from tarps and tents to a nice place where he could wine and dine $1,000 guns," said Tom. "Mike helped me some but I did most of the building. It was our routine to get up early, drive around looking for elk, then I'd work all day and we'd go scouting again in the evening. If we wanted to see lots of elk, we generally drove Waterman Road and the elk were in the hay fields. There were some really nice bulls."

Tom was still working on the cabin when archery season opened in August. Mike and Tom spent their mornings and evenings hunting on the nearby 101 Ranch and Tom recalled, "Mike said it was legal to hunt the 101 Ranch, but bow hunting wasn't allowed on other parts of the Collins' property. I found out later that Mike lied to me. Bow hunting was not allowed on any of the Collins' property. When I learned that I wasn't too happy because I could have gotten in big trouble for trespassing.

"Mike always was a talker, a big time talker. On several occasions he bragged he was buddy-buddy with Ringsage, the head detective on the Phil Brooks murder investigation. Mike claimed he was working with Ringsage to solve the case. It seemed to me Mike was overly eager to try and help the police. I do remember Mike telling me the caliber of the rifle that killed the cowboy. I just don't remember what caliber he said it was.

"In the end, Mike screwed me on the cabin. And I never did get to hunt the Fopiano, only that one time on the 101. I'm not the kind of guy who has to have a signed contract, but I'm old school enough I expect a man to live up to his word. When the cabin was finished, Mike tried to back peddle on our deal. I got some money out of Mike—it didn't pay the sweat equity I had into it—but at least it covered my expenses."

Eventually Detective Ringsage got around to interviewing Tom, grilling him for several hours about his dealings with Mike Williams. One thing he wanted to know was if Mike was prone to passing out and Tom said he had to laugh, that he never saw Mike pass out or even get light headed. Tom said he didn't know why the detective would ask him such a ridiculous question. Detective Ringsage asked Tom if knew where Mike was earning his living in 1994 and Tom said it appeared to him a pretty sizable chunk of Mike's income was coming from fee hunters on the Collins' property.

"I also threw in that I was always amazed at the toys Mike and Roetta had," said Tom. "They seemed to have a lot for what little bit of work they did. One time I was invited over to the Williams' house in Redmond to watch a hunting video. They were both on the video. It had been filmed on the Fopiano and Roetta shot a big, beautiful bull that was in the 350 range. Watching it she got all teary-eyed and afterward Mike said that was the last bow hunt on the ranch, that after that Jack Rhoden and Fran Cherry got together and forced the Collins' to outlaw bow hunting. He was pissed about it, said it cost him at least twenty grand a year when they took away bow hunting."

⊕ ⊕ ⊕

Johnny Rhoden, the oldest of Jack's two boys, was in Bend the morning after Phil Brooks was murdered. He was having a lift kit installed on his pickup at High Desert Four-Wheel Drive, owned by Rob Williams. While the mechanic was working on his rig, Johnny walked into the adjacent store,

185

Mountain Country Sporting Goods, and visited with Rob's stepbrother, Mike.

"A time or two in the past I had traded guns with Mike and he seemed pretty knowledgeable when it came to firearms," said Johnny. "We visited a little, and knowing he was an avid bow hunter, I asked him why he wasn't hunting. He said he had just come in from hunting the night before and was going back out. We talked some more and when Mike found out my dad was having surgery, and that I wanted to see how he was doing, he offered to run me to the hospital.

"The next time I saw Mike was at Sixshooter during the second elk season. That was real unusual for him to drive to our cabin. I don't remember him ever doing that except that one time. Mike started talking to Dad and I about the Phil Brooks shooting. He said he knew the caliber of the rifle that killed Phil. Said it was a 7MM. I remember Dad asking him if he was sure, and Mike shook his head up and down and bragged he had an in with the state police and knew for a fact it was a 7MM.

"Later that season, Dad ran into Mike along Waterman Road and stopped to visit. Dad said something about Mike having said it was a 7MM that killed Phil and Mike got all defensive, turned himself inside out denying he had ever said a caliber. He made such a big deal about it that Dad asked me if Mike had told us at Sixshooter what the caliber of the gun was that killed Phil. I said, yeah, it was a 7MM, and Dad said, 'Well now he's denying he ever told us.' I said that was a bunch of bullshit."

⊕ ⊕ ⊕

Rick Root had worked as a police informant for the Central Oregon Drug Enforcement team, as well as the Wheeler County Sheriff's Office. He came forward with information concerning Mike and Roetta Williams. Rick, who at one time had been related by marriage to Mike Williams and had hunted and traveled with the Williams' on numerous occasions, stated they often camped on public ground and trespassed on private property to hunt deer and elk. He recalled Mike being an excellent marksman and remembered Roetta favoring a .280 caliber rifle. He also remembered Roetta's rifle had been customized and the wood stock was replaced with a black synthetic stock.

"Before Mike and Roetta were married," related Rick, "they were driving on Highway 97 and got into a heated argument. Mike stopped the vehicle and Roetta got out and began walking away. Mike retrieved a pistol, shot in the air and fell down as if he had shot himself. He did this to get Roetta's attention, and so she wouldn't leave him."

⊕ ⊕ ⊕

Mike Williams used Wasmundt's Gun Shop in Fossil, the county seat of Wheeler County, to repair and customize the family's rifles. When Jim Washmundt looked at his repair log he discovered, between the years 1989 to 1991, Mike had brought eight rifles to be repaired at his gun shop that were within the caliber range in which the Oregon State Police crime lab indicated could have fired the fatal bullet that killed Phil Brooks. Two of these rifles were .280 Mountain Rifles.

⊕ ⊕ ⊕

Gene Adams was an avid hunter and a regular at Mountain Country Sporting Goods where he liked to talk guns and swap stories with Mike Williams. He recalled admiring a .280 Mountain Rifle and being impressed when Mike boasted about having worked up a new hot load for the .280 that allowed a 150-grain bullet to have the same velocity and killing power as a 7MM Magnum.

"One time I was in the store telling Mike about calling in a big six by six bull so my dad could take pictures with his camera," said Gene. "This was during archery season and I had already filled my tag. The bull was in the 320 class, not huge but nice, and I called him away from his cows and got him within 10 or 12 yards from Dad. The bull bugled and grunted, paced back and forth and whizzed on the ground. I had him all worked up and Dad got some great photos. When Mike heard my story he wanted me to take him to the spot the following morning.

"I stalled. I wanted to trade a hunt for a new stock on my rifle. Mike agreed and the next morning I took him to where I had called in the bull. But the elk had moved out and the only thing I was able to raise was a calf that began mewing, answering my calls. Mike wanted to know what that sound was, and that shocked me because every experienced hunter knows what sounds a calf, a cow and a bull will make. We hunted all that day and Mike was perfectly content to tag along behind me while I played guide.

"When it came time for Mike to fill his end of the bargain, he slapped the cheapest plastic stock they make on my rifle and called it good. It was junk. I threw it away and bought a better stock. I guarantee, that experience with Mike didn't leave a real good taste in my mouth."

Gene testified before the grand jury that during the 1990s Mike and Roetta were hunting with both rifles and bows. He also related a story about a big bull that had been killed on the Collins' ranch, saying, "Roetta was guiding a fee hunter. It was a great bull, 7 by 7, and at first they claimed it was way over 400 and a new state record. It turned out they measured wrong. It was closer to 370, but he was still a dandy.

"I looked at the photographs of where the bull was killed, recognized the landmarks and knew for a fact that spot was in the Fossil Unit. I also knew an Ochoco Unit tag had been used. I talked to Bob Collins about it. He confirmed an invalid tag had been used but said that was good because attention would be focused on the Ochoco and not the Fossil Unit. It's not right, to do something like that. In fact, using an invalid tag is strictly against the law."

Gene said he talked to Mike about the Phil Brooks murder and Mike said the fatal bullet had been recovered from the body. Because of his extensive experience with firearms, Gene said he did not automatically assume, as most people had, that a slug from a high-powered rifle, fired at a hundred yards, would blow right though the victim's body. He told a story of a five-point buck he killed at less than a hundred yards, hitting the animal just behind the shoulder with a .270 and 130-grain bullet, saying, "The slug never hit bone, only meat, and mushroomed. When I skinned the buck, the slug fell out. It was just under the hide on the opposite side from where I hit him.

"If I was asked whether a man could be shot at a hundred yards with a .280, or a 7MM, and not have the bullet blow through, I would say it's not very likely, but it is possible. There are a huge number of variables: the size and weight of the individual, whether it was a factory load or a short load, and on and on. Such a thing is way more common at 400 yards but you can't rule out a closer shot not exiting the body.

"I've noticed this about hunters, there are very few who can consistently make a 400-yard shot, especially and hit the ten-X spot. It is one thing to have a bull in your scope, and I would imagine it's quite another to have a man. It would take a certain individual who could remain calm enough to make a 400-yard shot on a human target. I'd guess only a handful of people are capable of doing something like that."

In Gene's estimation, Mike was a very competitive hunter. He claimed Mike often passed up quality animals for the opportunity to get an even bigger trophy. "He was always after a record," said Gene. "I've taken animals that would make the record books and never bothered to enter them. Horns are not that important to me. But for Mike, a trophy gave him bragging rights. That's the way he figured it. Bigger was always better with Mike."

⊕ ⊕ ⊕

The Kelly brothers, Greer and Tim, had their camp made on private ground south of the Fopiano. They had hunted the

189

several thousand acres owned by logger Craig Woodward of Prineville for a number of years, and 1994 was no exception. Hunting private ground afforded them privacy and there was room for two or three hunters but any more, in their opinion, was pushing it.

The evening of September 21st, 1994, the day after Phil was killed, the Kelly brothers were sitting in front of their tent in lawn chairs, relaxing after a long day of elk hunting. The campfire was blazing and they were drinking orange juice and vodka and eating peanuts, throwing the shells into the fire. It was a beautiful, star-studded night and the eastern sky was beginning to lighten in anticipation of the moonrise. All was quiet. And then the roar of an engine became audible and headlights danced and skittered through the timber. They had company.

"Mike and Roetta Williams showed up pulling a camp trailer behind their pickup," said Greer. "We had our tent on a little knob above Fry Creek, under a pine tree, and there was plenty of room for Mike to have parked away from us, but he didn't. He jockeyed the trailer around so close it almost touched our tent. That sort of pissed me off. I mean, one minute my brother and I are enjoying the peace and quiet and the next we are invaded. There was just absolutely no call for Mike to do what he did."

After Mike unhooked and leveled the camp trailer, he stepped over to the Kellys campfire and informed them he had permission from Craig Woodward to hunt the same private ground they were hunting. This irked Greer, as Mike backing his trailer so close to their tent had also irked him, but he held his tongue. They talked about hunting the property, and it was decided they would hunt together the following morning.

At daybreak on September 22 the four hunters began hiking. They reached a small clearing and Mike set himself and Roetta in front and had Greer and Tim stay behind as he began cow calling. He switched reeds, bugled and was immediately answered by a bull. It came crashing through the brush, and when it was within a few dozen steps from Mike, he stuck the bull with an arrow.

The hunters sat around munching on candy bars and waited for the bull to lie down. After an hour they took up the trail, finding round spots of blood here and there on the dry ground. But when the bull's tracks mixed with other elk and the bleeding stopped, they lost the track. Finally Greer and Tim offered to see if Joe Fitzgerald, a local rancher and known as the best tracker around, could come, lend a hand and find the bull before the meat spoiled in the heat of the afternoon.

"We drove to Joe's place," said Tim, "but he wasn't around. Ellen, his wife, told us Joe was off looking for a cowboy who was missing on the Fopiano. I asked her to relay the message to him we had a bull down and needed some help tracking. She said she would pass it on when he came in. She didn't know when that might be."

Greer and Tim returned to where the bull had been wounded and tried unsuccessfully to locate the tracks. They informed Mike and Roetta that Joe Fitzgerald was off looking for a lost cowboy on the Fopiano, and didn't know when, or if, he would be able to help find the bull.

That evening Mike and Roetta invited the Kellys to have dinner with them. They served lasagna and French bread. The brothers drank their screwdrivers, the Williams' did not drink, and according to Greer the conversation was lively with Mike doing most of the talking. In the wake of having shot a big bull he seemed especially gregarious, almost giddy. Roetta, in Greer's opinion, was reserved. But then again, Greer said he really didn't know her and had only met Mike a time or two.

Assuming Mike and Roetta would continue to search for the wounded bull, Greer and Tim hunted alone the following day, September 23rd. They returned to camp from their morning hunt, again drove to Fitzgerald's ranch and were informed the lost cowboy, Phil Brooks, had been found and he was dead from a gunshot wound. Upon returning to camp and finding Mike and Roetta at their trailer, Greer told them the news about Phil Brooks and the couple immediately announced they were driving to the Fopiano. They jumped in their pickup and sped away.

During the afternoon hunt, Greer noticed an odd shape under a pine tree and told Tim it looked an awful lot like an elk lying down. He looked through his binoculars, gave a short whistle and announced, "There's Mike's bull." It was a tremendous bull, a 6 by 6 with heavy horns and thick bases. It was a trophy, but the heat of the day had caused it to bloat and the meat was spoiled.

"It wasn't until four years later that Detective Ringsage questioned me about what had happened in 1994," said Greer. "And he was pushy—demanding to know dates and times and what went on when Mike and Roetta camped next to us—to the point I felt uncomfortable and finally asked if I needed to get a lawyer. After that, Ringsage eased up a little, but still I didn't like his aggressive attitude. It felt like I was having to defend myself."

At the grand jury inquest, Greer testified that Mike and Roetta Williams had never camped with him and his brother, either before, or after 1994. He was asked if it seemed as though the Williams' were trying to establish an alibi by parking so close and Greer said that very thought had crossed his mind.

⊕ ⊕ ⊕

Joe Kelly, Greer's son, attended Redmond High School and was a teammate on the 1994 football team with Grant Williams, Mike and Roetta's son. After most Friday night home games, Joe drove to Craig Woodward's property so he could bow hunt with his dad and uncle on the weekends.

Joe was subpoenaed to testify before the 2002 Wheeler County grand jury. The DA asked if Joe could recall whether Grant, who had said he hunted with his parents the weekend of September 17th and 18th, had returned to school and participated in football practice on Monday, September 19th. Joe shrugged and said he didn't know.

"I was hoping you would remember," said Tom Cutsforth. "Because that is the only reason you were called here today. You may go."

Joe got up to leave and then sat back down and faced the jury. He said, "I want to say something about hunting ethics. I think it's vitally important to have good hunting ethics. From what I know about Mike Williams, he has no ethics. He doesn't care about property lines and fences. He trespasses. Another thing, the one time Mike hunted with my dad and uncle, he crippled that big bull and didn't do everything he could do to find it. He let the meat spoil. And then he went back up there and cut off the horns. That's all he cared about, the horns."

Joe went on to explain that in 1994 Mike had invited him to stay at the Williams' camp and hunt the Fopiano during deer season. It was during this time that Joe said he observed Mike's lack of hunting ethics, going on to say Mike had crossed fences onto private property without the landowner's permission. Joe said that just wasn't right.

⊕ ⊕ ⊕

Joe Fitzgerald was well respected in the Central Oregon ranching community and renowned as a tracker. His voice was as gravely as a sack of rocks being shaken and he appeared as though he could have stepped from the big screen of a John Wayne movie. When the search party was being organized it was Joe who was elected to head up the cowboys.

"I didn't want to do it," growled Joe. "I told 'em no, but someone had to be in charge. I told the riders to fan out and we'd make a sweep of the country. But the Indian trackers stopped us before we ever got started. They wouldn't let us go no farther. That was on the second day. That was when they found Phil's body.

"I knew Phil pretty well. We rode together that spring bringing in cows and working cows. He was kind of a wild kid, Phil was, did more harm to himself than anybody else. I got along with him. I think all he needed was to grow up a little, but now he's never gonna get the chance."

After Phil's body was found, Joe returned to his ranch, checked the heifers, and since his horse was already loaded in the stock truck, he drove to Craig Woodward's property to look for the bull elk Mike Williams had wounded. It didn't take him long to find the track and blood sign. He stayed with it for more than a mile and located the bloated carcass under a tree. The meat was ruined and stinking. The horns had been cut off.

When Joe testified at the grand jury hearing he brought along his daily diary in which he recorded the low temperature for each day, as well as a summation of what he had accomplished. He read through the entries from September 19th to the 25th, noting the morning temperatures were generally in the 40 to 50 degree range.

The district attorney asked if Joe thought the killing of Phil Brooks could have been a case of mistaken identity and Joe bristled. "You might be blind, but you don't mistake a man and a horse for an elk. So, what I want to know is who the hell shot him? What was the motive? If Phil had been dogging somebody's wife, the husband wouldn't chase him down in the woods; you'd shoot him in the bedroom. And if this was over elk, well, I can't imagine a man getting killed over an elk."

One of the jurors asked what Joe thought of Mike Williams and he responded, "He's a blowhard who has never worked a day in his life. I caught him trespassing on me. People do that all the time. I don't think much about it. I just asked Mike not to do it again. But he never paid no attention to me. I've seen his boot tracks back up in there nearly every year. He keeps crossing the fence onto my property.

"As far as the killing, I'll go along with what Sheriff Otho Caldera said; he said, 'If I done this thing and it was an accident, my shirt won't touch my back before I told someone about it.'

"Nothing anyone can ever say is ever gonna convince me this was an accident. If it was, the person who done it has had plenty of time to come forward. No, this was cold-blooded murder."

⊕ ⊕ ⊕

Members of the Wheeler County grand jury had a number of questions for timber man Craig Woodward. They wanted to know if Mike Williams had the combination to his gates and Craig said he did. Craig was asked if he had ever had a conversation with Mike Williams about Phil Brooks.

"Yeah. I was at a bull sale when Mike came up and started gossiping in my ear," drawled Craig. "I'm not much for gossip. I tried to ignore him, but what I remember him saying was that a friend of his with the state police had told him the caliber of the gun that killed Phil was a .280. I remember that because a .280 and a 7MM are basically the same round, and half the rifles in this country are 7MMs."

Craig was asked how many acres he owned in Wheeler County and he said he really didn't know, anyway if he did know he sure as hell wasn't going to answer such a personal question. Asked if he considered Mike Williams to be a friend, Craig shook his head no and when the follow-up question was why did Craig allow Mike Williams to hunt on his property Craig replied, "Mike Williams gave me some information one time that helped me close a business deal. I was just returning the favor. I didn't know he was going to hunt on that particular piece of property where Greer Kelly was hunting. Greer didn't like sharing it with Mike, and he bellyached about the way Mike was trespassing on the neighbors. I finally had to tell Mike if he was going to hunt on me to stay on the other side of Buck Point Road. That eliminated the problem."

⊕ ⊕ ⊕

"Mike Williams is a shirttail relative of mine, but I don't like the guy and don't claim him as kin," said Bobby Ordway.

"To be honest, I wouldn't trust him as far as I could throw him. He's a thief. He stole pictures from me.

"When my dad died, Mike and Roetta came over to the house to give their condolences. I showed them my picture albums, one had a real nice 350 bull I'd killed with a bow on the Fopiano, and when my back was turned, they swiped the album. They used my photographs to promote their hunting. I know this as fact because Jim Peterson, a dentist and friend of mine from Prineville, was at a sportsmen's show in California. He recognized the photographs and called Mike on the carpet. Mike denied it, but he was lying big as hell.

"What he did with my photographs, passing them off as his own, was pretty much adding insult to injury. I had been dealing with Jimmy and Bob Collins on obtaining the hunting rights to the Fopiano, and Mike and Roetta swooped in and stole them out from under me. That sort of underhanded dealing doesn't set too well. Not with me. And especially after I'd taken Mike under my wing and showed him how to hunt the property. And did he listen? Hell no, he never listened.

"One time Mike and I were hunting and he crossed over onto Jack Rhoden's property to go after a bull. Bigger than shit he crossed the fence and he knew better because I told him so. He isn't beyond trespassing to get a trophy bull. He goes nuts when he's after a big set of horns, and Roetta is 10 times worse than he is.

"When Mike gets on an elk he stays with it all day. I told him to hunt early mornings and late evenings, let the bulls rest up during the day. Not Mike. He keeps after them and invariably pushes the bulls off the Fopiano and onto the neighbors' property where they're not hunted as hard. He cuts his own throat."

⊕ ⊕ ⊕

Roetta Williams was called to testify before the Wheeler County grand jury. A woman reserve deputy ran the metal detector wand over her to make sure, as they had on every witness who climbed the steps to the third floor courtroom, she was not armed. The alarm squealed. Roetta flippantly remarked, "It's probably just my nipple rings."

Digging a can of snuff from the hind pocket of her jeans, Roetta casually flipped it to her husband. And this time, when the wand was passed over her, it did not make a sound. Roetta, walking beside her attorney, climbed the stairs to the courtroom where the grand jury was eagerly awaiting her testimony.

In less than 10 minutes Roetta's boots could be heard clomping down the stairs and when she turned on the landing and started down the last run she looked up and flashed Mike a smile, acknowledging something, maybe it was a bond between them that they now shared. When she reached him, Mike handed her back her chew. She opened the can and took a dip, skillfully packing it under her bottom lip. Mike's name was called and he resolutely climbed the stairs.

Even before Mike had finished appearing before the grand jury, rumors were flying. But this time the rumors were not groundless. Mike and Roetta Williams, when called to testify about any involvement they might have had in the death of Phil Brooks, had pleaded the Fifth Amendment, allowing them to refuse to testify on the grounds they might incriminate themselves.

Roetta remained calm, almost stoic, but Mike, upon his return, was red faced and his bald head showed a thin sheen of sweat. As they were accompanied outside by council, a bystander tossed a caustic comment in their direction, "You guys either got the worst legal advice of all time, or you got something to hide. This don't look good."

The attorney glowered. Mike and Roetta stared straight ahead. When they reached the outside, Roetta spit in a flowerbed. They spent a moment talking to their attorney and then walked to their white pickup truck, the one with the vanity plate that read "6 by 6", and departed Wheeler County.

⊕ ⊕ ⊕

Keith Baker made several trips to the site on the Fopiano where he had found Phil Brooks' body. This was a case he wanted to solve. He thought the answers were there and that if he looked hard enough he would uncover them.

One time, as he was coming off the ranch and onto Waterman Road, Roetta Williams chased him down in an extended cab four-wheel drive pickup. She had four hunters with her. Mike, with more hunters in his pickup, showed up at about the same time and parked in front of Keith, effectively cutting him off from leaving.

"Roetta jumped out and was very pushy," said Keith. "She wanted to know who I was and what I thought I was doing on the property. When I told her, she demanded to know what I had found. I said I was just looking around. But what caught my attention was that she and Mike had shown up at nearly the same time, coming from different directions, and they had intercepted me. I knew they had to be in communication with each other, and noticed on the dash of Roetta's truck, was a radio headset. It was the type of device you wear on your hip and a wire goes to the headset. I realized they must use radios to communicate as a normal part of their hunting activities. I also thought, given that, if they had been involved in Phil Brooks' death, and I'm not saying they were, it could have been as simple as one person radioing another saying we've been spotted and he's headed in your direction. Do whatever you have to do to stop him.'

"I know that is probably an illogical assumption for someone to make, but on the other hand, if the Williams' were caught with a fee hunter, or they were poaching, they stood to lose their lease, their livelihood, their hunting licenses and the way of life they held so dear. Face it, people have been killed for a lot less—their pocket change or simply because of the shirt they were wearing.

"Back when we were kids we all played cowboys and Indians. You get shot, fall down, count to 10 and get up. But most people, when you actually shoot somebody and they don't get up, that event stays with you. It's not an easy thing to get rid of. I know this from having served as a sniper in Vietnam. I've had a hard time dealing with it. It's the realization that you took a life and a lot of times it's not something a killer lives well with."

⊕ ⊕ ⊕

Roetta Williams, the snuff dipping big game guide who had been raised in rural Oregon and knew all too well about subsistence living, flat refused to be interviewed by law enforcement. She left that to her talkative husband, Mike, and when he first spoke to Detective Ringsage about the Phil Brooks homicide, he happened to mention he and Roetta, "we were probably out bow hunting," when the murder occurred.

Mike later recanted that story. He next said he and Roetta had been at home in Redmond the evening Phil was killed. A day later, when Greer Kelly informed Mike and Roetta a cowboy was missing on the Fopiano, they never offered to search for the missing man, even though they knew the ranch and the layout of the land better than anyone.

Mike claimed the first he heard of the murder was from rancher Joe Fitzgerald. But Joe testified he never saw Mike during this time frame. And Mike claimed he and Roetta had driven to the 101 and had talked with Bob Collins. But this could not be true either, because Bob Collins testified he and his wife had gone to the coast on vacation and did not return home until Saturday, September 24th.

Another important fact was revealed when, as Detective Ringsage was bringing out Phil's body on Thursday, September 22nd, he encountered Mike and Roetta less than a half-mile from where Phil was killed. It was after dark. Hunting was not allowed on the Fopiano during bow season. And yet nobody thought to ask the Williams' why they were driving on that road at that time of the night. In fact, Detective Ringsage did not even make a note of the incident in his field notes.

It is suspected the Williams', including fifteen-year-old son Grant and Mike and Roetta, were hunting on the weekend prior to Phil being killed. Sheriff Dave Rouse examined the phone records. He stated, "There were no calls made from the home of Mike and Roetta Williams between the 16th through the 18th of September. Calls resumed on the afternoon of Sunday the 18th and sporadic calls were made for the next three days. On the afternoon Phil was killed, a call was made at 4:29 p.m. from the Williams' home to High Country Four-Wheel Drive. At 8:27 a call was made to Prineville hunting guide Stan Rodgers, and at 8:58 a call was made to the Clackamas home of Mike Williams' parents.

"I have to wonder if the first call could have been placed by Grant, looking for his father, but Mike said he was absolutely certain he made all three of the phone calls, and he admitted Roetta would not have placed any of those calls. Based on the phone records, and what Mike said, it does not appear Roetta was at home on the day Phil Brooks was murdered."

In fact, no one can recall having seen Roetta between the 16th and the 21st of September when she and Mike suddenly showed up in the dark, pulling a trailer and parking obnoxiously close to Greer and Tim Kelly's camp. When asked if he had hunted with his son and wife the weekend prior to the death of Phil Brooks, Mike claimed he could not remember if he had hunted with them, or even if he had hunted at all.

School records indicate Grant Williams was most likely in school on Monday, attended his classes that week, practiced football and played in the game on Friday night. When Mike Williams was asked about where he was from Sunday through Wednesday he said, "I felt my alibi was established because of the phone calls I made from home. When I was asked by law enforcement about those calls, I admitted I was the one who made them."

Scott Reed, who was married to Roetta's sister, stated, "Roetta said she and Mike were in Redmond on September 20th and they didn't even go hunting until the next day when they camped on public land with Greer Kelly. They went hunting the next morning and never found out about Phil Brooks until the following day."

After Mike and Roetta refused to testify before the grand jury, citing their Fifth Amendment rights, District Attorney Tom Cutsforth seemed at a loss on what his legal options might be. He talked over the case with the Oregon Attorney General's office, and it was decided to grant Mike immunity from prosecution in any matters relating to the death of Phil Brooks, thereby forcing him to appear and testify before the grand jury. In his testimony, Mike stated Roetta never hunted alone, but then he quickly changed his mind and said, "I suppose there have been times she could have hiked from camp and gone up on the ridge with a gun. I guess I couldn't say never."

Mike also swore under oath that Roetta did not serve as a hunting guide, anyway, he said, "Never on her own." However, Keith Baker observed her with hunters in her rig when she ran him down to question him about what he was doing on the property. And Larry Youngs stated, "Roetta showed us the ribbons the cops had staked out. Actually my son killed his elk on that same trail where the kid was killed. Roetta was guiding us at the time." And Gene Adams testified, "Roetta was guiding when the big bull, the one said to be a new state record, was killed and illegally tagged with an Ochoco tag in the Fossil Unit."

⊕ ⊕ ⊕

Questions surfaced about whether Roetta or Mike had a .280 rifle, the same type of rifle used to fire the fatal bullet that killed Phil Brooks. Mike admitted to having given a .280 Mountain Rifle to Roetta as a gift. Tony Conti, an employee of Mountain High Sporting Goods, operated by Mike Williams, said he ordered a .280 Remington Mountain Rifle through the store for Mike in 1984, and that Mike gave the rifle to Roetta. Mike said he sold that rifle to Tim Hargraves of Redmond in 1986.

However, there is evidence linking Mike and Roetta to a second .280 Mountain Rifle. Scott Sabo, who began working at High Country Four-Wheel Drive in the fall of 1989, testified he saw a .280 Mountain Rifle with a black composite stock and that Mike Williams said it belonged to his wife. Rick Root, the police informant who was a shirt-tailed relative of Mike Williams stated, "Roetta preferred a .280 caliber rifle for hunting and changed bullet weight for deer and elk." Gene Adams, a customer of the sporting goods store, said Mike Williams bragged to him about a special load he had developed for a .280 Mountain Rifle that shot a 150-grain bullet with a velocity comparable to a 7MM Magnum. District Attorney Tom Cutsforth said, "Mike Williams continues his lies. He has to separate his wife from that second .280 Mountain Rifle he built for her in 1989. We don't know where it is. It has never been accounted for."

Wheeler County Sheriff Dave Rouse, conducted a search with metal detectors under the meat poles at both the Rhoden's cabin on Sixshooter and the Williams' hunting cabin on the Fopiano. The sheriff thought he was likely to find a bullet where harvested game animals were hung, skinned and quartered, believing a bullet might have fallen unnoticed on the ground. The search revealed no likely matches from the Rhoden's property, but several .284 caliber bullets were recovered from the ground under the Williams' meat pole. Ballistics revealed that one bullet in particular was nearly a perfect match, with only minor variation in striations to differentiate it from the weapon that killed Phil Brooks. A ballistic expert said he could not say with absolute certainty that the murder weapon had fired both bullets. But then again, he said it might have.

When Mike Williams was asked if he had discussed with his daughter Jennifer, her testimony to the Wheeler County grand jury that her mother, Roetta, had hunted with a .280 rifle in the 1990s, Mike said that at no time had he and his daughter ever discussed her testimony at the inquest.

During 1992, when the stock of Mountain Country Sporting Goods was being liquidated, Mike Williams took a Remington .280 Mountain rifle to Jim Wasmundt's Gun Shop in Fossil for repair. It is not known what happened to this weapon but John King, foreman of the Wheeler County grand jury, said,

"Mike Williams stated under oath that neither he nor his wife owned any .280 or 7MM rifles in the 1990s."

⊕ ⊕ ⊕

Another piece of incriminating evidence possibly linking the Williams' to the death of Phil Brooks are tires. Keith Baker tracked the person he thought fired the lethal round to where a full-sized pickup truck had been parked beside a brush pile. He noted the distinctive tire tracks were identical to the tread from Les Schwab Wild Country tires. He estimated those tires had been driven less than a thousand miles.

Scott Sabo, employed as a mechanic at High Country Four-Wheel Drive, testified that in mid September 1994 he mounted a new set of Les Schwab Wild Country tires on the 1984 Ford crew cab pickup truck belonging to Mike and Roetta Williams. He recognized the design from photographs taken at the crime scene. Two years later, Keith Baker discovered vehicle tracks at the same brush pile with identical tread design as those he had observed at the crime scene, which lent credence to the fact the possible killer still had access to the property, and for all intents and purpose, it was, "business as usual."

⊕ ⊕ ⊕

On January 20th, 2002 Wheeler County Sheriff Dave Rouse and a number of officers had served a surprise search warrant at the residence of Mike and Roetta Williams, located at 3080 NW Euston Lane in Redmond, Oregon. The home looked more like a barn than a house, with a green tin hip roof and a loft as a living residence. The purpose of the search warrant was to locate and take as evidence any rifles that could possibly match the murder weapon in the Phil Brooks homicide, as well as any ammunition, bullets or other material used in reloading that might be traced back to the Brooks case, and records of any gun sales or guns that had been bartered.

"We didn't find much in the way of evidence," claimed Sheriff Rouse. "I will say that Roetta seemed extremely agitated when I told her I could account for Mike's whereabouts on September 20th but I could not account for where she had been. She flew into a fit of anger and said, 'We didn't know the kid. We never saw him. We don't even know what he looked like.'

"And later, one of my deputies overheard Roetta whisper to Mike, 'What if they find something we don't know about?'

"I felt that was a telling comment," said Sheriff Rouse. "We also found numerous firearms, even though Mike Williams had said they owned very few. He had also told me the family did not like the taste of wild game, but their freezer was chock-full of game meat."

Evidence generated from the search warrant, as well as other evidence gathered though interviews and a lengthy investigation, had led District Attorney Tom Cutsforth to convening the special grand jury. And after all the testimony, and Mike and Roetta Williams invoking their Fifth Amendment rights, one juror lamented that the DA, or any member of the grand jury, had not asked Grant Williams two important questions, "Did your mother stay in camp when your father took you back to Redmond?" and "Was your father in Redmond on Tuesday evening September 20, 1994?"

This juror went on to state, "If anyone had come forward to say they saw Roetta in the Mitchell area around the time Phil Brooks was murdered, we would have indicted her for murder. I think there is enough circumstantial evidence that she would have been found guilty."

⊕ ⊕ ⊕

Tom Cutsforth, after having granted Mike Williams immunity from prosecution in the death of Phil Brooks and forcing him to testify before the grand jury, felt that Mike Williams, during his guarded testimony, had lied under oath on several occasions. Charges were brought forward and the grand jury indicted Mike Williams on two felony counts of perjury.

The first count of the indictment stated Mike Williams knowingly made a false sworn statement when he said his wife did not own a rifle in the 1990s. The second count was whether Mike Williams lied when he said he never told Jack Rhoden, and his son Johnny, the caliber of the bullet that killed Phil Brooks.

⊕ ⊕ ⊕

The Brooks family was gathered to hear testimony in the perjury trial of Mike Williams. They sat in the gallery, on the wooden benches in the historic Wheeler County Courthouse and waited. Original oil paintings depicting abandoned homesteads and local landmarks, framed in rustic barn wood, decorated the walls.

Mike Williams, flanked by his attorney Tom Howes, entered the room through the double doors. Mike was dressed casually in blue jeans and a red shirt. His attorney wore brown slacks and a sports jacket the same green color as given to the winner of the Masters Golf Tournament. The attorney pushed open the swinging gate, went to the defendant's table, sat down and began arranging his papers.

Perhaps it was preplanned, or maybe Mike suddenly felt a stab of remorse for the suffering of the Brooks family, but at any rate he walked to where the Brooks family was sitting, lowered himself to one knee in front of Jim Brooks, and even though Mike had previously stated he never met Phil Brooks, would not know him from Adam, he cheerily said, "Hi there, Mr. Brooks. My name is Mike Williams. You've probably heard a lot of negative things said about me, but I just want to let you to know I knew your son and he was a great kid."

Jim Brooks, wearing a new pair of jeans with the cuff rolled up, cowboy hat resting on his knee, said nothing. He continued to stare straight ahead. After a long moment of uncertainty,

Mike Williams rose, and looking rather dispirited he went and sat beside his attorney.

On command, everyone in the courtroom rose. Circuit Judge Paul Crowley entered the room like a fresh breeze blowing down off the eastern flank of the Cascade Mountains. He was young, thin-faced and his rimmed glasses seemed to soften his hawkish features. He would have fit in as a professor at an Ivy League school but his looks and mannerisms made him conspicuous in cowboy country. The judge took his seat, scooted his chair to a small wooden table and the perjury trial of Mike Williams got under way. Roetta, who was outside the courtroom in the company of private investigator Rich Little, was conspicuous by her absence.

It was a warm day and a pair of old ceiling fans gently stirred the air overhead with boringly slow rotations. Judge Crowley dutifully read the charges, noting they were both Class C Felony Perjury offenses and carried a potential sentence of up to five years in prison on each count. "But realistically, under the current Oregon sentencing," said Judge Crowley in a voice as convincing as a used car salesman, "the actual sentence could be substantially less."

District Attorney Tom Cutsforth began his opening statement. He noted, "This case arises out of a 2002 Wheeler County grand jury inquiry into the shooting death of Phil Brooks that occurred in 1994. Nearly 100 witnesses were called before that grand jury. The grand jury had a great deal of difficulty with one witness who appeared before them, that witness is the defendant in this case, Mike Williams.

"When Mr. Williams took the stand he was granted immunity from anything except perjury because he had invoked his Fifth Amendment rights at that time. He took the stand and said he told Jack and Johnny Rhoden that the caliber of the weapon used to shoot Phil Brooks could have been anything from a .22 to a .338 Magnum. In other words, about any rifle ever made. And that is what he said from the witness stand. The trouble with that testimony is that Jack Rhoden took the witness stand and testified to a different story; that within 60 days of the shooting he said the defendant came to his cabin and told him Phil Brooks was killed with a 7MM slug. A 7MM is shot out of a 7MM rifle or a .280 rifle. Jack's son, Johnny Rhoden, happened to be present and overheard that conversation.

"The state will also show the defendant related the same story to Craig Woodward. At that time, only law enforcement knew the caliber of the murder weapon and they had been sworn to secrecy. That information was not released until a search warrant was served on Mike Williams in 2002 and made public.

"Mike Williams also told the grand jury his wife, Roetta Williams, did not own, possess or hunt with firearms in the 1990s. The state will prove that statement is false."

The first witness called in the case was John King. He had been the foreman of the grand jury. The District Attorney asked Mr. King to relate the testimony Mr. Williams had given to the grand jury about his conversation with Jack Rhoden at the Sixshooter Ranch in November 1994.

"Mike Williams' testimony was that he did not tell him the caliber of the bullet," said John King. "That he did not know the caliber that was used. He said he knew nothing about it and in his conversation with Mr. Rhoden he did not say anything about range or caliber."

The district attorney asked, "Do you remember me questioning Mr. Williams whether his wife owned or possessed a firearm in the 1990s? And what was his response?"

To this question John King answered, "Mike Williams testified they quit rifle hunting in the mid-1980s because they had to be in the sporting goods store during the busy rifle season. He said Roetta sometimes went hunting with family, and when she did, she used a .257 Weatherby. He also said he had a .280 rifle built for her in the 1980s but that he sold this rifle to Kevin Hargrave. After that he said they did not own any other .280 or 7MM rifles in the 1990s. He said his wife did not have a weapon of that caliber in the 1990s."

Sheriff Dave Rouse was called to testify the slug that killed Phil Brooks was a .284 and could have been fired from any rifle between a .280 and a 7MM. The next witness was Jack Rhoden, and when the DA asked him how his health and memory were, Jack responded, "Fairly good," but it was evident from his trembling hands and quavering voice that he was not a well man. On that particular day his dementia held the former mill owner and one of the wealthiest men in Central Oregon, in its sad, iron grip. When asked if he would recognize Mike Williams, Jack responded yes. When asked if Mike Williams was in the courtroom, Jack said he didn't think so.

"Do you remember having a conversation with Mike Williams at your cabin?" asked the DA.

"Yes," responded Jack. "We were going to take out some of the paid hunters. Ronny took them out. Johnny stayed with me. This was at Sixshooter Ranch. I remember the conversation with Mike Williams. He talked quite a bit. I don't recall too much what he said."

It was obvious Jack was not lucid enough to answer any more questions and the judge allowed him to step down. Johnny Rhoden was called to the stand and he remembered details of the conversation he and his father had with Mike Williams. He said, "It was the day before elk season opened, the second season so it would have been in early November. We had fee hunters there and Ronny was inside the cabin helping fix dinner. Mike drove in, got out of his pickup and we stood near the propane tank and visited. We talked about the weather, it was starting to get cold, whether we had seen any big bulls, we lied back and forth about that which is pretty common among hunters and guides, but mostly Mike wanted to talk about Phil Brooks and the investigation. He wanted to know what we knew, which wasn't much, and he bragged he knew the caliber of the rifle that killed Phil, that a friend of his in the state police said it was a 7MM.

"I remember that because I said something to the effect Ronny had a 7MM but my uncle Lee had driven over it with a jeep and it had never shot right after that. We laughed about it."

Timber man Craig Woodward testified he had been at a bull sale in early 1995 and Mike Williams came and sat down next to him and wanted to talk about Ronny Rhoden's possible involvement in the murder of Phil Brooks. Craig said he did not like gossip nor was he interested in discussing the investigation because Ronny was a friend of his. He categorized the conversation as one-sided, with Mike doing the bulk of the talking.

"Mike volunteered it was a .28 caliber that killed Phil Brooks and that struck me as odd he would know a specific caliber. I asked him about it," offered Craig. "Mike told me he had friends in the state police."

Scott Sabo again testified about the composite rifle he had seen at Mountain Country Sporting Goods in 1989, and that Mike Williams had said it belonged to Roetta. When Scott Reed was called to the stand he was very evasive and was quickly dismissed. Next to testify was Senior Trooper Todd Hoodenpyl, the Fish and Wildlife officer with the state police assigned to Wheeler, Gilliam and Morrow counties. He said his research into hunting records indicated that during the 1990s Roetta Williams had applied for more than fifty hunting tags for bighorn sheep, Rocky Mountain goat, bear, antelope, buck deer and bull elk. He said the majority of those hunts were designated as rifle hunts. The district attorney asked that this information be listed as state exhibits 1-3, and thinking he had made his case, Tom Cutsforth announced the state rested.

Tom Howes mounted a spirited defense for his client, attacking the wording of the first indictment in relation to the question of whether Mike had lied when he said Roetta never owned a rifle in the 1990s, Mr. Howes maintained that ownership and possession are vastly different in definition and meaning and that hunting with a rifle did not require ownership of that rifle. As character witnesses the defense attorney called two men to the stand, but they had known Mike less than seven years and had little to offer. Finally Mike Williams was called to testify, and after a few preliminary questions Mr. Howes got down to the business of defending his client.

"Did you ever own a sporting goods store?" asked Mr. Howes.

"No," said Mike. "My parents owned the store. I worked there from 1982 until it closed in 1992."

"How long have you been married to Roetta?"

"I better get this right," said Mike with a thin-lipped grin. "Thirty-two years."

"Are you familiar with guns and bullets?"

"Yes."

The defense attorney consulted his notes and asked, "How are you so sure that Roetta did not own a rifle in the 1990s?"

"Because she didn't know anything about rifles," said Mike. "I bought all the rifles. I would build a rifle, give it to her and say this is what you are going to shoot, and she would say great; show me where the safety is. I owned rifles in the 1990s, probably 10 rifles. If Roetta used a rifle it would more than likely have been one of mine."

"When did you and your wife start bow hunting?"

"That would have been in the 1980s," said Mike, "because it was very hard for us to get away from the sporting goods store during rifle season."

Again Mr. Howes consulted his notes. He asked, "Did you tell Jack Rhoden the caliber of the bullet that killed Phil Brooks?"

"I did not."

"Who was in attendance at that meeting?"

"Jack Rhoden and Johnny Rhoden. Ronny Rhoden came out of the cabin and sat on the steps but was not within hearing distance. We talked about hunting and Jack was always wanting to know information, what was happening over at our camp and what was going on as far as the state police investigation. If he asked a question, I guess I'd try and answer it to the best of my ability.

"There were all kinds of rumors, all kinds of stories and I talked to a lot of people and heard everything from it was a drug deal and they flew an airplane, heard everything. I passed along what I had heard about the bow hunters. But I didn't say anything about the caliber of the bullet. It was Jack Rhoden. He was the one who told me the caliber of the bullet. He said he knew because he had a friend in the police department."

"Are you friends with Jack Rhoden?" asked Mr. Howes.

"We have no relationship," said Mike coolly. "He doesn't care to have us next to him hunting. We are not friends. I've never confided personal information to him or his sons."

In his closing argument, Tom Cutsforth said, "Mike Williams testified in the grand jury inquest, and he testified again today, that he did not know the caliber of the bullet that killed Phil Brooks. Mr. Jack Rhoden was unable to testify because of his dementia. But his son Johnny was standing right beside him and did hear what was said, that it was a 7MM slug. The only person who could have known that at that time was law enforcement, the shooter or someone directly related to the shooter.

"Mr. Craig Woodward, who is not affiliated with the Rhodens and who has no animosity to the defendant, clearly testified that essentially the defendant was pestering him at a bull sale about this case and he didn't want to listen to it, didn't want to hear it, but the defendant not only told him the caliber but also the rifle, a .28, which is shorthand for a .280. Nobody, including law enforcement, knew that it was a .280 rifle that killed Phil Brooks. The only person that would have known that was the shooter, or someone directly related to the shooter. By telling these people the caliber of the weapon, Mike Williams fingered himself. When law enforcement came and talked to him, Mike refused to say he knew the caliber because if he knew the caliber he knew the shooter.

"Mike Williams uses words like 'never' or 'never ever' or 'didn't ever' that are broad and general; like his wife never hunted by herself, but then he backed away from that. He has to continue his lies, and he has to separate his wife from that other .280 Mountain Rifle. One rifle she received as a gift in 1984. It was sold in 1986. But Mike had another .280 Mountain

Rifle built for her in 1989. Scott Sabo saw it. He talked to Mike Williams about it in 1989. If I could conclusively put her in possession of that second .280 Mountain Rifle on September 20, 1994 this would be a different trial. I can't prove that she had possession of that rifle on that date. But circumstantial evidence indicates she had a rifle, possessed a rifle. That rifle was in her husband's gun cabinet. If he owned it, she owned it as a wife owns half of what her husband owns. Therefore, if Mike owned a rifle, and he has testified he did, Roetta owned half of that rifle. Where is that .280 Mountain Rifle, the second one? We don't know. It has never been accounted for.

"Sometimes we can't erase the things we've said. All of us wish we could. Sometimes we can't erase the things we've done, and we wish we could. Mike Williams opened his mouth, put both feet in, and got in front of the grand jury and committed perjury."

When it was Tom Howes turn to speak he scoffed at the state's evidence. In his closing remarks he went over what he claimed was a *fact* and said it was Mr. Rhoden who conveyed to his client the caliber of the bullet that killed Phil Brooks, and not the other way around. Then he read the definitions of "own" and "possess" from the Webster's Dictionary and concluded by saying the state's prosecution was "a case of wishful thinking" and there was no proof his client had committed perjury.

When the talking ended, all eyes in the courtroom shifted to the bench, where Circuit Judge Paul Crowley had his glasses off and was chewing thoughtfully on an earpiece. He took a deep breath, exhaled completely, drew another breath and began to speak.

"It is up to the state to prove a case beyond a reasonable doubt, the highest burden of proof in the world, and that is to prove to a moral certainty and that is the same burden of proof that applies in a death penalty case when a jury is asked if a person should be put to death. So, this is a very heavy burden.

"With respect to Count One—the allegation of perjury with respect to Ms. Williams' ownership of a rifle in the 1990s—I do not find that the state has proven the charge beyond a reasonable doubt. The reason for that is there is credible evidence from Mr. Sabo that he saw a rifle in 1989 that was claimed to be Ms. Williams'. But given the nature of the sporting goods business, and the inventory being used by family members, it is plausible that if the rifle did exist in 1990, and that it was used by Ms. Williams, it could technically not be *owned* by her. There is a big difference between ownership and possession. The indictment does not say possession; it specifically states ownership.

With respect to Count Two—it is interesting that Mr. Cutsforth paraphrased a statement that first came to light in the Watergate hearings, the question is what did Mr. Williams know and when did he know it. That was the critical issue in Watergate, which is what was asked of Mr. Nixon, what did he know and when did he know it.

"Given that the grand jury was investigating the death caused by a gunshot, and given that Mr. Williams was a potential suspect, in fact the sheriff used the word *primary* suspect, what Mr. Williams knew about the cause of the death and when he knew it are material to this case. There has been discussion about corroboration, and as I've thought more about this, Jack Rhoden did remember a conversation at the cabin and other parts of his memory failed, but his son gave specific information regarding the conversation and I think those two statements corroborate each other as does that of Mr. Woodward.

"I sat here within seven or eight feet of each witness. I looked at body language; the eyes, the breathing and things of that nature. I took into consideration that you, Mr. Williams are on trial for a very important matter. Here is the bottom line. I believed the witnesses, but quite frankly, Mr. Williams, I did not believe you. I do find the state has proven the second charge and find you guilty of perjury, a Class C Felony."

⊕ ⊕ ⊕

Tom Howes asked to negotiate a deal in regards to the perjury conviction of Mike Williams. Those negotiations concluded with an agreement between the parties that Wheeler County would dismiss the perjury conviction against Mike Williams in return for Roetta agreeing to submit to a polygraph test.

A polygraph test was immediately scheduled, but Tom Howes requested more time for his client. The test was rescheduled for the following month. It was assumed by some members of law enforcement that Roetta used the additional time to take a private polygraph test, and that she did not perform well on that test, because she failed to keep her appointment and meet with the state polygraph examiner at the scheduled meeting. A call was placed to Tom Howes. He stated, "Roetta is not going to take your test."

Mike Williams, convicted of a Class C Felony, served 90 days in jail, was fined $1,000, required to complete 120 hours of community service and given 36 months probation. He was not allowed to own, possess or carry a firearm. But after completing his sentence, the felony conviction was reduced to a misdemeanor and Mike Williams was again allowed to carry a weapon and to hunt. During Mike's incarceration, phone records between he and his wife held many interesting statements. One of those statements was Roetta asking Mike, "Do you feel any different now?"

⊕ ⊕ ⊕

To date, no person has been charged in the murder of Phil Brooks, and no person has come forward to admit any involvement in his death. The case remains open and active. For Phil Brooks, whose body lies at the end of an old cow trail in the cemetery on the Fopiano Ranch, and for his family, friends and all those who have been involved in this case, true justice remains elusive.

THE END

Epilogue

Mike & Roetta Williams—live in Bend, Oregon and still refuse to be interviewed by any member of law enforcement or the media.

Grant Williams—On October 4, 1997 Grant Williams was cited for spotlighting and killing a deer in Crook County. The weapon used to commit the crime was a .280 Mountain Rifle. Law enforcement recovered the bullet as evidence but ballistic tests were never done to exclude the rifle as the weapon that killed Phil Brooks. After the case came to trial, the bullet was destroyed.

Jack Rhoden—died in 2005 at age 80. The Sixshooter Ranch was sold to a California land speculator.

Ronny Rhoden—lives in his hometown of Prineville and continues to have occasional problems with his drinking and run-ins with the law. After the death of Phil Brooks, each time a photograph of a Rhoden family member appeared in the newspaper, Ronny received a copy of the article in the mail with crosshairs drawn over the photograph. A former member of law enforcement was implicated in sending these threats. He flunked a polygraph examination and had his DNA matched to the notes, but he was never arrested or brought to trial.

Jim Brooks—died of prostrate cancer in 2009 without ever knowing who murdered his son.

Joyce Brooks—lives on the family ranch near Mitchell and has never removed the memorial photographs of her murdered son from the wall by the door.

Tina Bolton—lives in Madras and continues to hope her brother's killer will have the courage to come forward and confess.

Justin Brooks—lives in Eastern Oregon and remains a cowboy.

Keith Baker—lives at Gateway, Oregon where he is involved in veterans' affairs. He is no longer able to track because of his service-connected disabilities from serving in Vietnam, but he still teaches tracking classes.

Dave Rouse—resigned as Wheeler County Sheriff, spent three years in Afghanistan and currently resides in Idaho.

Clyde Tankersley—lives in Central Oregon and has had several more convictions for drug and alcohol related crimes.

Detective Robin "Robb" Ringsage—although it is difficult to gather information from a closed society like the Oregon State Police, an organization that protects its own at all costs, it appears Detective Ringsage was demoted in 2000 and worked game violations in Baker County until he retired from the force.

Dale Kielhorn—has never been heard from again.

Rick Steber, the author of thirty books and sales of more than a million copies, has received national acclaim for his writing. His numerous awards include the Western Writers of America Spur Award for Best Western Novel, Western Heritage Award, Benjamin Franklin Award, Mid-America Publishers Award, Oregon Library Association Award and Oregon Literary Arts Award. Two of his books have been optioned to movie production companies.

In addition to his writing, Rick is an engaging Western personality and has the unique ability to make his characters come alive as he tells a story. He has spoken at national and international conferences and visits schools where he talks to students about the importance of education, developing reading and writing skills, and impressing upon them the value of saving our history for future generations.

Rick has two sons, Seneca and Dusty, and lives near Prineville, Oregon. He writes in a cabin in the timbered foothills of the Ochoco Mountains.

Special Thanks

To Dianne Van Swoll and her tireless efforts at editing my work. And to my friends who also help with suggestions, constructive criticism, editing and encouragement. Thank you all....